Coffee, Cookies, & Inspiration

Other Books by Mary Hampton

A Tea for All Seasons
Tea and Inspiration

If you are interested in having Mary Hampton speak to your church,
organization, or special event, please contact:

The Write Connection
1535 NE 86th Avenue
Portland, OR 97220
Telephone: 503-251-8678

Zondervan Gifts would like to thank J.C. Penney's Housewares Department located in Woodland Mall, Grand Rapids, Michigan, for the generous loan of most of the place settings used in this book, and

Vance and Karen Forshey of the Madison Street Inn for the use of their Queen Anne–styled home as a setting for a number of the pictures shown in this book. You can call them at 616-459-5954 for a reservation.

We would also like to thank Lynne and David Swets for allowing us to photograph the rest of the shots in their 1907 historic Georgian Revival home. Their house was restored in 1993 and is an ongoing project. Both homes are located in the historic Heritage Hill District of Grand Rapids, Michigan.

MARY PIELENZ HAMPTON

Coffee, Cookies, & Inspiration

Heartwarming Moments with God

A COLLECTION OF DEVOTIONS & RECIPES

ZondervanGifts

We have a gift for inspiration™

Coffee, Cookies, & Inspiration
Copyright 1998 by Mary Pielenz Hampton

ISBN: 0-310-97205-1

All Scripture quotations, unless otherwise noted, are taken from the *Holy Bible: New International Version* (North American Edition). Copyright 1973, 1978, 1984, by International Bible Society. Used by permission of Zondervan Publishing House. All rights reserved.

The "NIV" and "New International Version" trademarks are registered in the United States Patent and Trademark Office by International Bible Society.

Published in association with the literary agency of Alive Communications, Inc., 1465 Kelly Johnson Blvd., #320, Colorado Springs, CO 80920

Senior Editor: Gwen Ellis
Design: Veldheer Creative Services & Sherri L. Hoffman
Art Design: Patti Matthews
Photography: Bob Foran
Requests for information should be addressed to:

Zondervan Publishing House
Mail Drop B20
Grand Rapids, Michigan 49530
http://www.zondervan.com

Printed in China

99 00 01 02 /HK/ 9 8 7 6 5 4 3 2 1

To Joy Marple and Gwen Ellis,
my coffee-loving editors,
with thanks for the inspiration and
realization of this book.

Contents

Introduction

Be Warmed and Be Filled

*C*hildren's laughter. A touching story. The first rose of spring. A newsy letter from a faraway friend. An unexpected good deed or kind word. The aroma of freshly baked cookies. The warmth of a perfect cup of coffee. A special time with God.

It's the simple things that fill our senses and warm our hearts. And though we plan big events and fancy affairs, it's often quiet moments that affect us the most. And those are the moments we're most likely to remember and share with others.

Coffee, Cookies and Inspiration is filled with opportunities for special moments. Inspirations gleaned from ordinary experiences are combined with cookie recipes and coffee suggestions to help create a special "coffee break with God." The inspirations are paired with Scripture passages that form the foundation for these special devotional times.

We often hurry through our time with the Lord the same way we gulp our morning coffee. *Coffee, Cookies and Inspiration* can be a savored oasis of refreshment that will help bring a new sense of warmth to our moments with God.

There are a number of ways to use this book. Make the cookies when there's time, then brew a special cup of coffee and enjoy both while reading the Scripture and the devotion.

Each recipe makes plenty to share with others in our lives. As we share the cookies with our families, a neighbor, or a co-worker, we can also tell them what we learned from the devotion.

I call the combination of a recipe with an accompanying Scripture passage "Food for Thought." I've used the "Food for Thought" method to reach women in my church, inviting them over for special treats, then sharing the message with them while we fellowship together and enjoy our refreshments. I also know of women who use it as a ministry to shut-ins, taking the treats to people in rest homes and sharing the devotional thoughts with them as well.

One church that invited me to speak used the devotion to open their weekly women's Bible study. After a time of worship and prayer, one woman read the devotion to the group. After the study, they served the food that corresponded to the lesson.

Coffee, Cookies and Inspiration can transform our coffee times into special devotional times. During these special times, our hearts are warmed and our spirits filled with the faithfulness of God, with his ability to reach each of us wherever we are in life as we allow him to shape us in his image.

Coffee: Legends and Locations

No one knows for sure who first discovered that the seeds of the cherrylike coffee fruit had many uses. Initially, Ethiopian nomads ground the seeds and mixed them with animal fat. They made them into small balls and carried them as rations—the first "energy bars." Other African tribes made a drink from the fermented fruit.

Around A.D. 1000, Arabian tradesmen brought coffee plants home. The first brewed beverage was _kishr_, which used the hulls of the fruit.

The truth of how our own roasted bean beverage came into fashion is unclear, but experts agree Arab countries were drinking coffee—more or less as we know it—by the fifteenth century.

Coffeehouses developed soon after, and the popularity of coffee began to spread to other Middle Eastern countries. By 1645 the first known European coffeehouse opened in Italy. At the end of that century, coffee could be found in most European nations. Even England, widely known for its preference for tea, readily accepted coffee around 1650. Coffee officially became the hot beverage of America following the Boston Tea Party.

Although coffee was native to the tropics of the Eastern Hemisphere, in the early eighteenth century a single coffee plant survived an ocean voyage with Gabriel Mathieu de Clieu, an infantry captain on the island of Martinique. He planted the tree among thornbushes. Four years later he distributed the seeds to people he thought would be able to provide the care required. There were nearly nineteen million coffee trees found on the island within fifty years. From Martinique, coffee was planted throughout the western tropics, adding new variety to the available crop.

A Mixed Bag

Although most coffee comes from a single species of coffee plant, _where_ it is grown greatly influences the taste of the coffee. Understanding the qualities inherent in the different beans will help you select a coffee with the characteristics you most enjoy. You can also create your own special blend by purchasing different coffees for their special traits and grinding them together for a custom cup.

Brazilian: Brazil is the largest producer of coffee beans in the world. Not particularly distinct, Brazilian coffee has a good medium body, is slightly acidic with a pleasant earthiness.

Colombian: Colombia is the second-largest coffee producer. Colombian coffee is full-bodied and richly flavored.

Costa Rican Tarrazu: The strongest tasting coffee produced in Central America. Tarrazu has a sharp acidity and heavy body.

Ethiopian Harrar: An unusual coffee that grows wild, Harrar is very aromatic and winey.

Jamaica Blue Mountain: A rare coffee noted for its mellow flavor and aroma, light acidity, and full body.

Java: A popular coffee with full body and rich, acidic, and slightly smoky taste.

Kona: The only coffee grown in the United States, it is a full-bodied coffee with a spicy, nutty sweetness that makes it very popular.

Mexican: A coffee with a pleasing aroma, rich flavor, and mild body.

Mocha: Grown wild in Yemen, known for its slightly chocolate aftertaste. There is a common misconception that a "Mocha Java" is simply a chocolate-coffee drink. True Mocha Java is a rare blend of the beans from these two neighboring coffee producers.

Sumatran: An Indian coffee that produces a mellow, rich cup with full body.

These are just a few of the common coffees you can choose. Your coffee supplier should be able to explain the characteristics of various beans.

Coffee: And So It Grows

Coffee beans are actually the seeds of the coffee cherry. These cherries grow on a tree that resembles a camellia, with dark, shiny leaves and jasmine-type flowers. While coffee trees can be grown ornamentally in many climates, those harvested for coffee production grow in the tropics in both hemispheres. Coffee cherries thrive in the rich, warm soil and gentle rainfall.

Although there are many varieties of coffee trees, more than ninety percent of commercial coffee comes from either *arabica* or *robusta* trees.

Arabica beans were the first coffee beans known to be used in a beverage. European travelers to Turkey, Syria, and Egypt discovered the coffeehouses in those countries during the sixteenth century. The beans they used were from Arabia. Today arabica beans are the more desirable coffee bean, producing higher quality coffees used by premium roasters. These beans have lower caffeine content and are somewhat more dense than their lesser-quality cousin, the robusta bean.

Robusta trees mature more quickly and will tolerate greater variations in soil quality, rainfall, sunlight, and altitude. They are also more resistant to disease. These factors make robusta coffee the logical choice for some of the poorer coffee-producing countries. The coffee produced from robusta beans is commonly found in ground, canned coffee on supermarket shelves.

From Cherries to Coffee Beans

Today coffee is harvested and processed in the same way it was five centuries ago. The coffee tree may show blossoms, green fruit, and ripe fruit all at the same time. Only the perfectly ripe fruit is suitable for coffee beans, so the fruit must be harvested by hand.

After the cherries are picked, there are two processing methods that can be used to separate the beans from the surrounding pulp and husk.

The more primitive method, dry curing, is still used for more than half of the world's coffee. Once picked, the coffee cherries are spread in the sun to dry. After fourteen to twenty-one days, a hulling machine strips the hulls from the now-dried fruit.

The wet-curing method involves delivering the just-picked fruit to a processing mill, where the pulping process takes place. First the coffee cherry is washed; then the seeds are squeezed from the pulp. Still encased in their parchment-like wrapping, the seeds are placed in water tanks for up to thirty-six hours. This loosens the papery covering, and the fermentation that takes place helps develop the flavor of the beans. Finally the beans are washed to remove the last bits of pulp and parchment and then dried either in the sun or in drying machines. The final product, green coffee beans, is ready for market.

The Art of the Roast

You may be thinking, "I've never seen a green coffee bean!" While green beans are available at some specialty coffee shops and roasters, most beans are sold already roasted.

Roasting may be the single most important variable in the taste of a cup of coffee. The roasting process gives a particular coffee bean its characteristic color. It also dictates which flavors will be evident.

Roasting is a matter of subjecting the green beans to intense, dry heat—four to five hundred degrees Fahrenheit. The remaining moisture is removed during this process, and the beans will crack (a sound similar to popcorn popping). This cracking noise signifies the beginning of the actual roasting of the beans.

The roasting process is watched carefully so the beans will achieve the desired characteristics. As the coffee bean roasts, the cellular structure of the bean begins to break down, releasing steam. The sugars caramelize within the bean, the oils inside the bean begin to be released, and some acids begin to form.

It helps to understand what takes place as the coffee beans roast, so you can choose coffees that have the characteristics you prefer.

I used to live about five blocks from a coffee roasting company. Twice a week I would smell the coffee roasting, even with the windows closed. It began as a pleasant scent, but at times my husband and I would joke that "they're burning their beans again." I didn't care for the smell, and I've found that I don't like my coffee with that burnt taste either.

Now that I understand more about coffee roasting, I avoid espresso roast altogether (that burnt flavor is the goal of espresso roast). I prefer a lighter roasting of the coffee beans, even though it isn't as popular in general.

A Roast by Many Other Names

The coffee industry has fairly standardized terminology, so once you know a little about roasting, you should be able to select the type of coffee you prefer without guesswork.

Cinnamon Roast: Considered the lightest roast worth making into a cup of coffee, cinnamon roasted beans are the color of a cinnamon stick—a light brown color—and have a dry surface. This coffee may also be called New England or light roast. Cinnamon roast coffees are not tremendously popular, because they develop a "toasted" flavor rather than a true coffee taste and can have a sour or acidic undertone.

American Roast: As the name implies, it's a typical roast in America. The beans have a medium brown color and a dry surface. The flavor is less like toasted grain than the light roast and has developed some sweetness and richness that balances the slight acidity.

City Roast: Slightly darker brown than the typical American roast, city roast has usually lost its acidity and developed more sweetness.

Full City: Probably the most common roast served in cafes around the country. It is noticeably darker than the standard American roast, with a richer coffee flavor. Often patches of oil have begun to show on the surface. If so, this roast may also be called light French.

Dark Roast: As the name implies, these beans are dark brown in color and now much of the coffee oil is visible on the surface. All of the acidity has been lost, and there is a noticeable bittersweet taste. There may also be a slightly smoky taste. Dark roast is also commonly called French roast.

Espresso Roast: Very dark, almost black in color, with a very shiny, oily surface. This coffee has a noticeable burnt taste that overrides the typical coffee tastes and smells. It may also be called Italian roast.

The particular roast you select affects more than just the taste of a cup of coffee. Lighter roasts are harder to grind to a fine powder, which makes them unsuitable for some brewing methods. The darker roasts are more brittle, which is why they can be ground into the fine espresso-style coffee.

If you're particularly adventurous, you can roast your own coffee at home. As I mentioned, green coffee beans are available at some specialty coffee suppliers, and there are even mail-order sources. The most successful home-roasting methods include using a petal-type vegetable steamer placed on a baking sheet in the oven or in a stovetop popcorn popper. There is one style of automatic popcorn popper that will work also.

It's very important to understand the process before you try it (using the wrong type of popcorn popper could be a fire hazard). I would recommend reading one of the books available on home coffee-roasting.

Coffee Shopping

Specialty coffees are increasingly available, and cafes and supermarkets now carry many varieties of bulk coffees. You usually have the option of grinding the coffee there or buying whole beans and grinding them at home. It's recommended that you purchase whole beans and grind them yourself to keep your coffee as fresh as possible. Also, the grinders available in most stores are not necessarily cleaned between coffees, so you might end up with an unexpected combination of coffee flavors.

If possible, ask the salesperson when the coffee was roasted. Coffee begins to stale as soon as it leaves the roaster, so it's much more desirable to have week-old beans than stale six-month-old beans. It helps to purchase your coffee from merchants who sell a lot of coffee. They're more likely to have fresh shipments arriving regularly.

Storage of coffee is another important consideration. Most coffee experts agree that putting coffee in the freezer is only necessary if you've purchased a flavored coffee that you won't be using quickly. Any coffee that is high in oil content is likely to turn rancid if stored for long. It's best to purchase about a week's worth of coffee and simply keep it in an airtight container.

Home Brewing

Once you've selected your coffee, you have many preparation options. First you will need to choose a grinding method.

There are essentially two types of coffee grinders—the blade grinder and the burr grinder. Blade grinders are generally much less expensive—you can often find them on sale for under twenty dollars. They may be described as "coffee and spice mills," which means they will grind spices and nuts as well as coffee. This can be an advantage when you want to add these to create your own flavored coffees. Unfortunately, a blade grinder doesn't produce a consistent grind.

The burr grinder is more expensive but yields coffee with a perfectly uniform grind. It is not recommended to use a burr grinder for anything other than coffee beans; therefore you can't grind spices or nuts along with your beans.

There are essentially four basic grinds, and each is suited to a particular brewing method. In general, the less time the coffee will be in contact with the water, the finer the grind needs to be in order for the full flavor to be extracted. Burr grinders are adjustable according to the desired grind, so there are no time recommendations.

Coarse Grind: Five to seven seconds in a blade grinder. Used for percolated coffee or for making coffee concentrate (a stovetop method in which the coffee grounds are boiled with the water and then strained out).

Medium Grind: About ten seconds in a blade grinder. Medium grind coffee is best for drip coffee with flat-bottomed filters, or a plunger pot—also known as a French press.

Fine Grind: Fifteen to twenty seconds in a blade grinder. Used for cone-shaped drip coffee makers and for Turkish coffee.

Extra-Fine Grind: Twenty-five to thirty seconds in a blade grinder. This is used for espresso machines.

Brewing methods are primarily a matter of personal preference, although expense can be a factor.

Percolator: Modern percolators can produce a delightfully rich coffee without the over-boiled taste of early percolators. The coffee grounds are placed in a mesh basket that fits into the pot. Water reaches the boiling point and is forced up a tube in the center of the basket. The hot water then drips through the grounds. Use coarse grind coffee in a perco-lator, since the water cycles through the grounds more than once.

Plunger Pot or French Press: A pot with a nar-row, straight-sided glass cylinder. Coffee and very hot (not quite boiling) water are placed in the cylinder, and then a tight-fitting, mesh screened plunger is inserted. After the coffee has steeped, the plunger is pushed to the bot-tom of the container, trapping the grounds and preventing the coffee from being over-steeped. It makes a rich cup of coffee and has the advantage of being small and portable. Use medium grind coffee in a French press.

Drip Coffee Makers: The drip coffee maker can be automatic or can resemble a glass beaker. Both use a filter into which the ground coffee is placed.

With an automatic drip machine, the water is placed in a tank, where it is heated and then dripped onto the coffee in the fil-ter. The coffee then drips into a carafe on a heated plate. In a nonelectric coffee maker, the water is heated to just below boiling in a kettle, then poured into the filter. The coffee drips into the bottom of the carafe, and when done the filter is removed and the cof-fee served from the carafe. Use medium grind coffee in an automatic machine that requires flat-bottomed filters, and fine grind coffee in the cone-shaped filters.

Ibrik: An ibrik is a specialty pot used for Turkish coffee. It is a long-handled metal container narrowed at the top, with a spout to pour the finished brew. Turkish coffee instructions can be found on page 17. Turkish coffee requires fine grind coffee.

Espresso Machine: Espresso machines use pres-sure to force the hot water through the cof-fee, resulting in a very concentrated brew. The original espresso machine is the Italian-style stovetop model that is still used in most Italian homes. It is inexpensive (under twenty dollars for a basic model), and although it doesn't produce enough pressure to satisfy many who desire pure espresso, it is good for producing a concentrate for cap-puccino or other milk-type drinks. The elec-tric models can create more steam pressure and thus a more concentrated espresso. Espresso machines must use the extra-fine grind coffee.

Electric espresso machines usually have an attachment for steaming milk used in cappuccino and latte drinks. There is now an inexpensive, manual milk frother on the market. The milk is heated and then poured into a plunger system that looks like a French press. The milk is whipped into a froth by moving the plunger up and down several times.

Coffee grinders and brewing equipment are increasingly available. You can usually find a good selection in the department store house-wares section. Many coffee suppliers and cof-feehouses also sell specialty coffee equipment. Also, mail-order companies sell coffee-brewing equipment as well as coffee beans. You can even join coffee clubs that automatically ship coffee selections to you. There is no need to settle for mass-produced grocery store coffee if you prefer something more exciting.

A Few Other Tips . . .

After you've selected the perfect coffee, ground it to the right texture, and chosen your brewing method, there are several other things to keep in mind.

As with any beverage, the finished product is only as good as the water used to make it. If you live in an area with very hard water or water that doesn't have a pleasing flavor, you may want to use bottled drinking water or springwater (not distilled). Or you may want to filter your drinking water.

After you've brewed your coffee, if it will not be consumed within about fifteen minutes, transfer the hot coffee to a thermal carafe. Temperature is very important to coffee flavor. Leaving the carafe on the heating element of a drip machine results in "overcooking" the coffee, making it bitter.

It's also important that all the equipment you use be as clean as possible. Be sure to thoroughly clean your coffee grinders, your brewing equipment, and your cup or mug.

Automatic equipment should be put through the recommended cleaning cycle on a regular basis to ensure that there is no residue on the interior pipes. Carafes and other equipment can be cleaned with a mixture of baking soda and water.

Stylish Service

Although coffee is often consumed on the run, the purpose of *Coffee, Cookies and Inspiration* is to make your time special, less rushed, more savored. One way to make it significant is to add special but simple touches that you might otherwise skip.

Choose something unique or beautiful to serve your coffee. There are many "coffee services" available. Most china patterns have coffee servers that match specific designs, or you can choose a fanciful one to your liking. Coffee servers resemble teapots, but they are usually taller, with a narrower neck, and more full at the bottom.

You can drink your coffee out of a plain mug, but there are many interesting items available as well. Earthenware is ideal for coffee because it retains the heat well. You can use a pretty china coffee cup, but be sure to warm the cup with hot water before filling it with coffee. This will help the cup retain the heat of the coffee. If you like any of the international-style coffees, such as espresso or Turkish coffee, there is usually a specific type of cup available for serving.

If you like your coffee lightened, warmed milk or half-and-half is best. For sweetening, there are many choices, including brown sugar or one of the specialty syrups sold at most coffeehouses. Whipped cream, mini chocolate chips, or a cinnamon stick also add nice touches.

Some Coffee Recipes

With the recipe that accompanies each devotion, I suggest a particular type of coffee you may want to try. The recipes for these coffees follow. If you prefer, you can use any variety and roast of coffee you enjoy. The proportions aren't as specific as those found in cooking recipes, because many of the ingredients can be added in amounts to suit your taste.

You will notice that some of the cookie recipes simply recommend a particular flavored coffee. While some coffee purists think flavored coffee is pedestrian, many others enjoy coffee that has flavored oils added just after roasting. There are many flavors available, from almond to vanilla.

If you don't want to purchase specially flavored coffees, you can make your own versions by grinding the recommended nuts or spices with your coffee beans. You can also add a few drops of a flavored extract to the water before you brew the coffee. Extracts can also be added to the final pot, but I prefer to let the flavors infuse the coffee itself rather than be added full strength at the end.

Cappuccino: Two and one-half espresso-sized cups of water, one tablespoon extra-fine grind coffee, one-half cup milk. Brew espresso using a stovetop or electric espresso maker. Steam milk using steamer attachment or heat milk and whip to foam with cylinder-style frother. Fill small cups with half espresso, half hot milk. Top with froth.

Cafe Caramel: Brew your favorite coffee. To each cup add one tablespoon of warmed, prepared caramel sauce. Stir thoroughly to dissolve. If desired, top with whipped cream and sprinkle with cocoa.

Cafe Mocha: This can be made using your favorite coffee. You can either add unsweetened cocoa to the ground coffee prior to brewing or add prepared chocolate syrup to each cup of coffee. Top with whipped cream or steamed milk and froth and sprinkle with cocoa.

Cafe Cinnamon: If you're using a blade grinder, break a cinnamon stick into pieces and grind with coffee beans. Brew coffee as usual and serve with a cinnamon stick stirrer.

Turkish Coffee: In an ibrik or small saucepan, heat one cup cold water to just warm. Add two teaspoons fine ground coffee and two teaspoons sugar. Stir and bring to a boil over medium heat. As coffee reaches boil, pour half into heated demitasse or Turkish coffee cups. Return remaining coffee to the boil. Remove from heat and spoon foamy coffee into cups. Do not stir. (You drink Turkish coffee grounds and all, so it is important to grind it as finely as possible.)

I hope you'll enjoy experiencing new types of coffee and trying new recipes, but most of all I hope you'll enjoy this unique way of meeting with God alone and sharing your love for him with others.

All things are possible with God. Mark 10:27

Endless Possibilities

Recipe: Afghans

A wife of noble character who can find?
   She is worth far more than rubies.
Her husband has full confidence in her
   and lacks nothing of value.
She brings him good, not harm,
   all the days of her life.
She selects wool and flax
   and works with eager hands.
She is like the merchant ships,
   bringing her food from afar.
She gets up while it is still dark;
   she provides food for her family
and portions for her servant girls.
She considers a field and buys it;
   out of her earnings she plants a vineyard.
She sets about her work vigorously;
   her arms are strong for her tasks.
She sees that her trading is profitable,
   and her lamp does not go out at night.
In her hand she holds the distaff
   and grasps the spindle with her fingers.
She opens her arms to the poor
   and extends her hands to the needy.
When it snows, she has no fear for her
   household;

for all of them are clothed in scarlet.
She makes coverings for her bed;
   she is clothed in fine linen and purple.
Her husband is respected at the city gate,
   where he takes his seat among the elders
   of the land.
She makes linen garments and sells them,
   and supplies the merchants with sashes.
She is clothed with strength and dignity;
   she can laugh at the days to come.
She speaks with wisdom,
   and faithful instruction is on her tongue.
She watches over the affairs of her household
   and does not eat the bread of idleness.
Her children arise and call her blessed;
   her husband also, and he praises her:
"Many women do noble things,
   but you surpass them all."
Charm is deceptive, and beauty is fleeting;
   but a woman who fears the LORD is to be
   praised.
Give her the reward she has earned,
   and let her works bring her praise at the
   city gate.

Proverbs 31:10–31

Endless Possibilities

Have you ever seen one of those Magic-Eye pictures? If you squint and make your eyes go blurry, you can see a different image hidden within the picture. That's how I like to look at the "Virtuous Woman" of Proverbs 31. Hidden in the picture of this role model of efficiency and accomplishment, there is another image that doesn't get discussed as often.

What first made me give this woman a second look was the fact that she had "servant girls." This lady had household help! I liked that idea. Beyond that, however, she was a woman who made the most of her time and found activities in which she excelled.

She's not simply a picture of the model homemaker. Taking care of her family was a priority, but this lady's life consisted of much more than cooking, cleaning, and baby-sitting.

She was a gourmet cook and a fine seamstress. She had a green thumb; she was a wise investor and a good businesswoman (even in a man's world). She was charitable, industrious, and wise. She was strong, confident, and happy.

She wasn't perfect, and I'm sure God didn't include her description to discourage or defeat us. On the contrary, I'm glad that God included this woman as an example of the endless possibilities open to women. The variety of her interests and activities are inspiring. God has given women so many skills and talents, and more opportunities to put them to use than ever before. The Rev. Stuart Briscoe said, "Some [women's] talents lie buried because they have never been unearthed. They have not been consciously buried. They simply have never been explored."[1]

Sometimes this woman's list of accomplishments seems beyond possibility for us to attain. But when I look more closely at this passage, I can see many ways we can each realize some of these same accomplishments.

Here are just a few possibilities: Child care services can be exchanged with a friend who could teach a new skill, such as sewing. College or adult education courses are available to learn about investing money. Many simple recipes are creative and expose our families to foods from other cultures. A passion for crafts can be turned into a profit. We can use our own creativity to come up with more possibilities.

Is there something in your heart that you've longed to pursue, but you've been afraid it didn't fit the picture of a godly woman? As you read Proverbs 31, take another look at your life and find a new way of viewing the endless possibilities God has given you.

Afghans

The name of this cookie reminds me of the woman of Proverbs 31, who "makes coverings for her bed." If you squint and make your eyes go blurry, this chocolate version of the traditional lace cookie looks like crochet. Serve Afghans *as a reminder of the endless possibilities God gives to women.*

½ cup (1 stick) butter, soft but not melted
½ cup brown sugar
⅓ cup light corn syrup
1 teaspoon vanilla extract
⅔ cup flour
¼ cup unsweetened cocoa
¼ teaspoon salt
1 cup rolled oats

Preheat oven to 350 degrees. Line baking sheets with parchment or grease generously.

In a medium bowl, use electric mixer on medium speed to beat butter, brown sugar, corn syrup, and vanilla until well blended. In a small bowl, stir together flour, unsweetened cocoa, and salt. Add to butter-sugar mixture and beat until smooth. Gently stir in oatmeal. Drop batter by level teaspoonfuls three inches apart onto prepared sheets (cookies will spread). Flatten slightly with the bottom of a glass. Bake five or six minutes or until edges begin to firm. Let cookies cool briefly on sheets, then remove to wire racks to cool completely. Store in airtight container. Makes three dozen cookies.

I like *Afghans* with *cafe caramel.*

Being confident of this, that he who began a good work in you will carry it on to completion. Philippians 1:6

Rainbow Promises

Recipe: Cloud Cookies

God said, "This is the sign of the covenant I am making between me and you and every living creature with you, a covenant for all generations to come: I have set my rainbow in the clouds, and it will be the sign of the covenant between me and the earth. Whenever I bring clouds over the earth and the rainbow appears in the clouds, I will remember my covenant between me and you and all living creatures of every kind. Never again will the waters become a flood to destroy all life. Whenever the rainbow appears in the clouds, I will see it and remember the everlasting covenant between God and all living creatures of every kind on the earth."

So God said to Noah, "This is the sign of the covenant I have established between me and all life on the earth."

Genesis 9:12–17

Some areas of the country are blessed with more rainbows than others. With rainy days more than one-third of the year, the rain-soaked states of Oregon and Washington have many rainbows. In southern California, however, they appear so seldom that they are traffic-stopping occurrences. I especially remember one particular southern California rainbow.

I had spent the weekend with my church youth group at an orientation for a spring break mission trip to Mexico. Although I had committed my life to Christ as a child, that weekend I felt, in a way I had never experienced before, the Lord's presence and promise to use me. Even in the middle of several hundred other students, I was completely alone before God. I felt him working in my heart, asking me to commit my life to him in a deeper way.

I was afraid that if I told anyone how I felt, they would tell me that I had got caught up in the excitement. I'd go home and everything would be just as it had always been. So I kept the experience in my heart.

The rain that had threatened to pour all weekend held off until we loaded the buses to go home. I was glad for the gentle grayness. The excited chatter of the trip to the retreat was replaced with quiet talk on our return. While the

Rainbow Promises

rest of the young people talked or slept, I sat looking out the window, talking with God and treasuring the experience I'd just had.

As we drove along near Burbank, a ray of light broke through the clouds in a silver streak, casting a brilliant rainbow that shone against the charcoal hills. It took my breath away. I glanced around to see if anyone else had noticed it. If they did, no one said anything. I didn't point it out to anyone, either. I felt as if this rainbow were just for me, a symbol that God would keep his promise to use me in a special way.

Just as Noah's rainbow was a marker of new life and a new relationship between God and his people, that day marked a beginning for me. It was the beginning of a heart committed to living for God daily. It was the beginning of a relationship with God that wasn't dependent on anyone else. It was the beginning of a recognition that I wanted to be used by God rather than using him for security, acceptance, love, or anything else. I haven't been the same person since.

The mission trip to Mexico that spring was exciting and challenging. I had thought maybe the trip itself was to be the fulfillment of God's promise to use me, but I think that moment between God and me during the orientation was the most important part of the whole experience.

I kept that experience to myself for almost twenty years. Sometimes when God works in our hearts or promises us something, it seems appropriate to share it with everyone else so that they may rejoice in seeing his work, too. At other times the message is so personal that to share it would seem to dilute the special moment. God doesn't always seal his promises to us in a visible way, like a rainbow, but once we've heard the message, there is no mistaking his voice.

Have you heard his promises to you? He promises you a new life—a new chance to live for him. Whenever you see a rainbow, take a moment to acknowledge his promises and look for the many ways he has kept his word.

Cloud Cookies

God set his rainbow in the clouds as a promise to never again destroy the earth by flood. These cloudlike cookies can help you remember that God will always keep his promises to you.

¾ cup (1½ sticks) butter, soft but not melted
½ cup sugar
1 egg
1 teaspoon vanilla extract
2 cups flour
½ teaspoon baking powder
½ teaspoon ground cloves
⅛ teaspoon salt
about 40 whole cloves
powdered sugar for rolling

Preheat oven to 350 degrees. Lightly grease baking sheets or line with baking parchment.

In a medium bowl, cream butter and sugar together until well blended. Beat in egg and vanilla until light and fluffy.

In another bowl, combine flour, baking powder, ground cloves, and salt. Add to egg mixture and mix until smooth dough is formed.

Form dough into 1½-inch balls (about ½ tablespoon of dough). Place on cookie sheets about two inches apart. Press one whole clove into top of each cookie. Bake for twelve to fifteen minutes or until lightly golden.

Remove from baking sheet, roll in powdered sugar and cool on wire racks. Cloves can be removed before serving. Store in an airtight container. Makes forty cookies.

Cloud Cookies are good with *hazelnut coffee.*

As for me, it is good to be near God.   Psalm 73:28

Taking a Creative Approach
Recipe: Almond Tile Cookies

One day as he was teaching, Pharisees and teachers of the law, who had come from every village of Galilee and from Judea and Jerusalem, were sitting there. And the power of the Lord was present for him to heal the sick.

Some men came carrying a paralytic on a mat and tried to take him into the house to lay him before Jesus. When they could not find a way to do this because of the crowd, they went up on the roof and lowered him on his mat through the tiles into the middle of the crowd, right in front of Jesus.

Luke 5:17–19

We're used to coming into God's presence at church, at the kitchen table with Bible, notebook, and study books spread out, or in beautiful places of his creation. But life can be filled with many obstacles that distract us from spending time with God. And at times the typical methods don't work, and the familiar places are filled with distractions.

The hassles of Sunday morning preparations linger and prevent us from entering into genuine worship at church. Or sometimes the roles we play as teacher, singer, usher, or helper use all our time and attention.

Sitting at the kitchen table might be one of the worst spots to try to be alone with God. The hub of the house is often filled with ringing telephones, grocery lists, dinner preparations, and dirty dishes, all calling for attention. Even when admiring God's creation, the babbling brooks, singing birds, and blue skies can fill our senses to the brim, leaving no room to notice his presence.

Often the obstacles aren't visible, like the crowds that kept the paralytic from Jesus or like children who need to be fed or mountains of work to be done. We can let noises—internal and external—keep us from hearing his voice. Letters to write. Daydreams and fantasies. Children calling. Music playing. Television blaring.

In her book *Home Is Where You Hang Your Heart*, Cynthia Culp Allen tells of moving to a large city with its many distractions. She found it difficult to find God with so many things competing for her attention. I found this to be true in the process of writing this book. We just moved to a large city, into a house that needs a lot of work before it will feel like home. New routines, a new church, new commitments all compete for my time and attention. I can't turn to the places where I comfortably sought God's presence before, because nothing is the same.

When the obstacles around us prevent us from approaching God in the usual way, sometimes we need to be creative and find a new approach. In one of our homes, my mom carved out her own quiet place in a corner of a closet under the stairs. It was an odd corner that had no shelves or racks for hanging clothes. A small window let in the afternoon sunlight. She outfitted the nook with a small table and a chair and called it her "prayer closet."

It wasn't like sitting at the kitchen table, in the middle of the hustle and bustle of the household. If she had her Bible or other study books out, she could leave them and return at her convenience. When the family wanted her attention, the closet wasn't an obvious place to look. In her prayer closet she could read or pray virtually undisturbed. The telephone could go unanswered, and there were no household distractions begging for attention—no piles of laundry beckoning, no dinner preparations calling out, no dusting or vacuuming whispering to her.

My mom isn't the only woman who has been resourceful in getting around the obstacles to being in God's presence. Susannah Wesley, mother of the preachers and hymn writers Charles and John Wesley (plus *seventeen* other children), used to raise her skirt up over her head to have some undisturbed moments!

Writer Heather Harpham Kopp tells of going out on the roof outside her bedroom window as a young woman to have time to herself. Anne Ortlund found that to have her time alone with God, she needed to get up in the middle of the night when the rest of the household was sleeping.

Does anything hold you back from approaching God? Sometimes there are just too many obstacles to go into God's presence the usual way. But with a little resourcefulness, you may be able to get there by the back stairs, out on the roof . . . or in the closet.

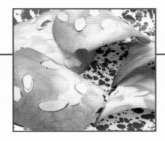

Almond Tile Cookies

These traditional cookies look like the roof tiles that might have been removed for the paralyzed man to be lowered into Jesus' presence. Serve Almond Tiles *and remember to be creative when getting around the obstacles that keep you from God's presence.*

2 egg whites
½ cup superfine sugar
⅛ teaspoon salt
½ teaspoon almond extract
¼ teaspoon vanilla extract
1 tablespoon butter, melted
¼ cup cake flour

Preheat oven to 400 degrees. Generously grease two baking sheets.

In a medium bowl, beat egg whites, sugar, salt, extracts, and butter on low speed until foamy. Sift in cake flour and gently fold into mixture.

Drop tablespoonfuls of batter about four inches apart onto greased cookie sheets. Spread batter into very thin circles, three inches each.

Bake, one cookie sheet at a time, for six to eight minutes or until edges are just browned and centers are golden.

Using a thin spatula, quickly remove from sheet one at a time and drape over rolling pin to shape. Repeat with rest of batter. Work with only four to six cookies at a time so you have time to form them. If cookies get too crisp to work with, return to oven for no more than one additional minute. To retain crispness, store cool cookies in a single layer in an airtight container. Makes 2½ dozen cookies.

Almond Tiles are delicious with *cappuccino,* but they're a special treat with a scoop of coffee ice cream.

*I will lie down and sleep in peace, for you alone, O L*ORD*,*
make me dwell in safety.   Psalm 4:8

The Heart's True Home

Recipe: Bird's Nests

How lovely is your dwelling place,
    O Lord Almighty!
My soul yearns, even faints,
    for the courts of the Lord;
my heart and my flesh cry out
    for the living God.

Even the sparrow has found a home,
    and the swallow a nest for herself,
    where she may have her young—
a place near your altar,
    O Lord Almighty, my King and my God.
Blessed are those who dwell in your house;
    they are ever praising you.

Psalm 84:1–4

This psalm is a beautiful picture of home in its truest sense. A place of safety—safe enough to bring precious children there. A place of rest—where the body is refreshed to continue with the daily chores of life. A place of provision—nourishment and comfort to build strength to face life's challenges. A place of sanctuary—where the deepest part of the soul longs to be.

What does your dream house look like? Is it a sprawling estate with rolling lawns and carefully cultivated gardens? Or a cozy cottage with chintz curtains and old roses? Maybe you dream of a weathered beach house with worn wood floors and faded wicker furniture? Or a secluded country cabin with a crackling fire and curious critters at the back door? If you have children, you may dream of a quiet neighborhood with safe streets and enough space both inside and out for them to play and explore, laugh and learn.

I dream of a house with as many windows as the walls will hold. Warm sun streaming in. Views of green hillsides or windswept beaches. Comfortable places for conversation, and cozy spots to curl up with a book.

At times I long for the home of my imagination: when I drive down our rocky, unpaved road; as the morning sun drifts around to the windowless part of the house; when opening the drapes on the window obscured by the neighbor's broken-down boat. When my world is dark and dreary or unfriendly and frightening, I find rest for my spirit as I envision the home of my heart. I can dream vividly enough to see rays of sunlight streaming through clean, clear windows. I can imagine lush morning glories growing along the tall fence outside my window. I hear lively conversations as friends and family gather in comfort.

The Heart's True Home

I've never lived in my dream house. But I have learned that there is a wonderful sense of comfort and peace and safety and security in the house of the Lord. The older I get, the more I appreciate this concept of dwelling in the safety of the Lord's presence.

When I was young, I often didn't appreciate the security of my family. Although I remember times of emotional, financial, and personal insecurity, there was an underlying sense of assurance that I'd be okay. As a child, I knew it wasn't up to me if the bills got paid or the car got repaired. I could rest in the care of my parents to keep me safe despite turbulent circumstances. Even when things were difficult at home, there was an underlying security in knowing that there was someone there looking out for me, wanting the best for me, protecting me from the storms of life.

Now that I'm grown up, though, I know I can't just go about my business and expect everything to be taken care of for me. As I learn to nest near God's altar, I can rest and know that Someone is still there, looking out for me, wanting the best for me, protecting me from the storms of life.

There is a famous photograph of a steep hillside with a roaring waterfall cascading down. A tree growing out from the side of the hill holds a bird's nest in its topmost branches. At first glance it would seem that the bird that chose this spot as its haven was the inspiration for the term "birdbrain." But a longer look reveals that the treacherous location of the tree offers protection from predators, while still being out of reach of the raging water.

To the outside world, resting in the Lord can look like "being out on a limb." Once you've experienced it, however, you find that the world can rage around you, but in God's home is a place of peace and safety that defies explanation.

Bird's Nests

These nestlike cookies can be a reminder that there's no safer place than the presence of the Lord.

⅓ cup butter
⅓ cup sugar
⅛ teaspoon vanilla extract
1 egg
1¼ cups self-rising flour
about ⅓ cup quick toasted, shredded coconut
candy-coated almonds

Preheat oven to 375 degrees. Generously grease a baking sheet.

Cream together butter and sugar until light and fluffy. Add vanilla extract and egg and beat well. Fold in flour until well mixed.

Make batter into one-inch balls (about ½ tablespoon of batter) and roll in toasted coconut. Place balls on greased baking sheet. Press center of each cookie with thumb to make slight indentation. Place two or three candy-coated almonds in indentation.

Bake for about ten minutes or until tops are golden and edges are very lightly browned. Cool briefly on baking sheet, then remove to wire rack to cool completely. Makes two dozen cookies.

Try these buttery *Bird's Nests* with *French-roast coffee* made in a French press.

Thy words became for me a joy and the delight of my heart; for I have been called by Thy name, O LORD God of hosts. Jeremiah 15:16 (NASB)

Going Deeper

Recipe: Moravian Spice Cookies

When the queen of Sheba heard of Solomon's fame, she came to Jerusalem to test him with hard questions. Arriving with a very great caravan—with camels carrying spices, large quantities of gold, and precious stones—she came to Solomon and talked with him about all she had on her mind. Solomon answered all her questions; nothing was too hard for him to explain to her. . . .

She said to the king, "The report I heard in my own country about your achievements and your wisdom is true. But I did not believe what they said until I came and saw with my own eyes. Indeed, not even half the greatness of your wisdom was told me; you have far exceeded the report I heard. How happy your men must be! How happy your officials, who continually stand before you and hear your wisdom! Praise be to the LORD your God, who has delighted in you and placed you on his throne as king to rule for the LORD your God. Because of the love of your God for Israel and his desire to uphold them forever, he has made you king over them, to maintain justice and righteousness."

Then she gave the king 120 talents of gold, large quantities of spices, and precious stones. There had never been such spices as those the queen of Sheba gave to King Solomon. . . .

King Solomon gave the queen of Sheba all she desired and asked for; he gave her more than she had brought to him. Then she left and returned with her retinue to her own country.

2 Chronicles 9:1–2, 5–9, 12

Now the Bereans were of more noble character than the Thessalonians, for they received the message with great eagerness and examined the Scriptures every day to see if what Paul said was true.

Acts 17:11

Going Deeper

*T*hink back to the time you first fell in love. Didn't you want to know *everything* about your new love? You wanted to meet his family and friends, see where he lived, and learn what was important to him.

The summer Dean and I met, we spent night after night talking until the wee hours of the morning, learning about one another. After a few months, I noticed that Dean started to visibly fade after 9:30 P.M. Being the night owl that I am, I sometimes wondered what happened to the guy who made it on six hours of sleep when we were just getting acquainted.

God probably wonders sometimes what happened to us. Once the newness of our relationship with him wears off, that initial excitement can turn into complacent contentment. We stop rising early or staying up late to be intimately acquainted with him.

God is revealed to us through his Word, the Bible. Just as a marriage needs time and attention to stay close and strong, so our relationship with God, our genuine first love, needs time and attention to maintain intimacy with him. It's a sacred opportunity that we often take too lightly.

If you'd like to search the Scriptures more deeply for yourself but don't know where to begin, try some of these methods:

Take notes during sermons at church, being sure to write down every Scripture reference the pastor mentions. Later look them up so you can see for yourself how the Scriptures support one another.

Go to the reference section at your local Christian bookstore. There you can find commentaries on specific books of the Bible that will give you greater background and insight. Cross-reference systems will help you locate other Scripture passages related to the one you are studying. You may also be interested in books that tell more about cultural aspects of biblical times.

It's also good to choose favorite passages of Scripture to memorize. Committing God's Word to memory will allow him to bring it to mind at opportune times.

You can go deeper in your study by listening to theologians and teachers on radio programs or when they are speaking in nearby communities. Many Bible schools and seminaries offer extension courses to the public. Often you can take them for enrichment with no other college training required.

Spending time to learn about God and what he has to say to you will bring you into a deeper, more intimate relationship with him. You may find that you fall in love with your true first love all over again.

Moravian Spice Cookies

The richness of the spices in these cookies can remind you of the treasures in God's Word. Enjoy Moravian Spice Cookies *while you search the Scriptures for yourself.*

½ cup (1 stick) butter, softened
¾ cup firmly packed dark brown
    sugar
1 egg yolk
¼ cup molasses
½ teaspoon vanilla extract
2 cups flour
½ teaspoon baking soda

¼ teaspoon salt
1 teaspoon ground cinnamon
1 teaspoon ground ginger
½ teaspoon grated nutmeg
½ teaspoon ground allspice or cloves
1 teaspoon finely ground pepper
    (preferably white)

In a large bowl, use an electric mixer on medium speed to beat butter and brown sugar until light and fluffy. Beat in egg yolk, molasses, and vanilla.

In a medium bowl, stir together flour, baking soda, salt, and spices.

Beat flour and spices together with molasses mixture until well blended. Refrigerate for at least one hour or until firm.

Preheat oven to 350 degrees. On waxed paper, roll dough into very thin (⅛ inch) rectangle. Using sharp knife or pastry cutter, slice into 1½-inch squares.

Place on ungreased baking sheets and bake for eight to ten minutes or until set but edges are not dark. Cool briefly on pan, then remove to wire rack. Store in airtight container. Makes eight dozen cookies.

The dark spiciness of *Moravian Spice Cookies* would go well with *any rich roast of coffee.*

*Not one of all the L*ORD*'s good promises to the house of Israel failed;*
every one was fulfilled.   Joshua 21:45

"Occupant Ready"

Recipe: Wasp's Nests

[The LORD said,] "I will send the hornet ahead of you to drive the Hivites, Canaanites and Hittites out of your way. But I will not drive them out in a single year, because the land would become desolate and the wild animals too numerous for you. Little by little I will drive them out before you, until you have increased enough to take possession of the land."

Exodus 23:28–30

[The LORD said,] "I sent the hornet ahead of you, which drove them out before you—also the two Amorite kings. You did not do it with your own sword and bow. So I gave you a land on which you did not toil and cities you did not build; and you live in them and eat from vineyards and olive groves that you did not plant."

Joshua 24:12–13

After more than four hundred years of slavery in Egypt, the children of Israel were going home. Not in the way you and I might think of home. After all, none of them had ever lived in the Promised Land before. They were going to a new home, and it would be a hospitable place. Israel didn't have to build homes or plant gardens when they got to the Promised Land. God had the previous tenants take care of that long before they got there.

Can you imagine how exciting it must have been to arrive in their first real home? Canaan was a beautiful new place where everything was ready and waiting.

God's promises in this passage became especially significant to me as I prepared to leave my home so my husband could go to seminary in Portland, Oregon. It wasn't as though I had always lived in one place. On the contrary, my family moved quite often when I was growing up. I didn't attend the same school for more than two years until I reached college. When we moved to San Luis Obispo in the middle of my senior year in high school, I wasn't very happy about it. But my mother was certain that God never called one part of a family without having a plan for the rest of them as well.

After a few years my parents moved away, but I had begun to put down roots in San Luis Obispo. I left to take jobs elsewhere for a couple of years and then returned in my mid-twenties to complete college. I realized that SLO (as it is affectionately known by locals) was the first place I really considered home. And somehow the older I got, the more important that became to me.

If it had been up to only me, I would probably have stayed there for the rest of my life. But when the time came for Dean to go to seminary, it was clear that we needed to move on. In the midst of our moving preparations, God used this passage to give me confidence that he would take care of the details just as he had for the Israelites.

As we began making plans to relocate, we found that we already had a number of friends in the area where we were moving. My former pastor and his wife, who had been like family to me for many years, lived there. Many writers with whom I was acquainted lived in the area, also. And a couple from our church in San Luis Obispo were also relocating to the Portland area within months of us.

God promised that the Israelites wouldn't have to build homes in their new land. We had missionary friends returning to the field who needed someone to rent their home.

God provided vineyards and orchards for the Israelites. For me, there was Trader Joe's, a discount specialty food store that became a favorite place for inexpensive foods and baking products. It might seem silly to be comforted by a specific market near my new home, but God cares about the details—even what we have to eat.

After seeing how God had prepared our new home for us, I couldn't help but laugh when Dean pointed out the wasp's nest under the eave of the house.

God clears the path and sets the scene. Whether it's a move to a new neighborhood, a new job, a new church, or a new family situation, we can be sure God not only has led us there but has prepared the way and established provisions for us.

Whatever new situation we may face, we don't need to be intimidated by the size of the adjustment we think will be required. Instead we can look for the creative ways that God has prepared everything we'll need.

Wasp's Nests

God used the symbolism of wasps (hornets) to describe how he drove the previous residents out of the Promised Land so the Israelites could come in and live in their houses and eat from their gardens. Wasp's Nests *can be a reminder that the Lord will give you just what you need in every new situation into which he leads you.*

1 cup lightly toasted almonds, ground
   fine
½ cup superfine sugar
1 tablespoon unsweetened cocoa powder
2 tablespoons confectioners' sugar

2 egg whites
⅛ teaspoon cream of tartar
½ teaspoon vanilla extract
½ teaspoon almond extract

Preheat oven to 325 degrees. Line baking sheets with parchment paper or brown kraft paper.

In a small bowl, mix ground almonds with two tablespoons of the superfine sugar. Add cocoa powder and confectioners' sugar and mix well.

In a medium mixing bowl, beat egg whites and cream of tartar on high speed until foamy. Gradually add remaining superfine sugar and continue to beat until mixture is glossy and stiff peaks form when mixer is lifted from bowl. Beat in vanilla and almond extracts.

Fold in cocoa-almond mixture just until blended. Spoon into pastry bag fitted with medium plain tip or cut ½ inch off the corner of a plastic sandwich bag. Pipe into mounds on prepared baking sheets.

Bake twelve to fifteen minutes, until firm to the touch. Cool on wire rack. Store in airtight container. Makes two dozen cookies.

Wasp's Nests are delicious with *mochaccino* (cappuccino with chocolate syrup added).

*"Am I only a God nearby," declares the L*ORD, *"and not a God far away? Can anyone
hide in secret places so that I cannot see him?"* Jeremiah 23:23–24

The Heavens Declare...

Recipe: Mocha Meringue Stars

Where can I go from your Spirit?
  Where can I flee from your presence?
If I go up to the heavens, you are there;
  if I make my bed in the depths, you are
  there.

If I rise on the wings of the dawn,
  if I settle on the far side of the sea,
even there your hand will guide me,
  your right hand will hold me fast.

Psalm 139:7–10

Robert Louis Stevenson wrote, "The moon has a face like a clock on the wall." Sometimes children talk to "the man in the moon." Some parents even tell their children that the man in the moon looks down over them at night so they won't be afraid of the dark. One child's bedtime prayer says,

I see the moon and the moon sees me.
God bless the moon and God bless me.

It's not surprising that the moon and stars remind us of God's presence. There seems to be a natural connection. Earthly glimpses of the heavens turn our thoughts toward God's dwelling place. God himself used a star to communicate his presence on earth to the Magi. A long time ago people believed that the Milky Way was a pathway into heaven for angels. It's even been said that the light the stars give comes from the glory of God shining through holes in the night sky.

Several years ago I had an experience that showed me how the heavens can make me aware of God's presence. I had worked at a Christian camp all that summer. It has never been easy for me to leave camp, and it was especially hard after a long summer living, working, and learning together with the same people. I had many significant experiences and developed some special relationships. When Labor Day came, there was a definite sadness as I watched my new friends begin their drive down the mountain to points all over California.

I wasn't going home quite yet. After spending a few days at a new friend's home, we'd return to my hometown, where we'd attend college. When we got down the mountain, I was feeling somewhat melancholy. While my friend busied herself visiting friends and getting ready for college, I had plenty of time to replay in my mind special moments from the summer. It was a little like being in suspended animation—I was no longer at camp, but I hadn't fully re-entered the real world, either.

My friend lived in the middle of California's Central Valley. The Sierra Nevada Mountains lie just to the east, but it's flat as far as the eye can see in every other direction. At night the sky seemed to stretch out forever. Late that first night I went out on the balcony and looked over the valley. I glanced up, with visions of dear faces and places flashing in my mind against the night sky. As I caught a glimpse of the nearly full moon, I realized that all over California the same moon was shining down on all the people who had become so important to me. And that the God who made the moon was watching over us all. In an odd way, that made them seem a little closer.

There is no greater comfort than in knowing that the Father of Light can see you clearly. Those times when you feel especially far from familiar places and loved ones, you can be sure that you have never gone so far that God is not with you.

Mocha Meringue Stars

These star-shaped cookies can remind you that you will never go so far that God's presence is not there.

> 2 egg whites
> ¼ teaspoon cream of tartar
> ⅛ teaspoon salt
> ⅔ cup sugar
> 1 teaspoon vanilla extract
> 2 tablespoons unsweetened cocoa powder
> 1 tablespoon espresso powder (not granules)

Preheat oven to 300 degrees. Line baking sheets with baking parchment or brown kraft paper.

In a large bowl, combine egg whites, cream of tartar, and salt. Beat on high speed until foamy. Gradually add sugar, beating until mixture is glossy and stiff peaks form when mixer is lifted from bowl.

On low speed, beat in vanilla. Add cocoa and espresso powders and beat until evenly distributed.

Fill a pastry bag fitted with a large star tip. Pipe into stars (about one teaspoonful) on lined baking sheets. Bake twenty-five to thirty minutes or until firm to touch but not browned. Let cool on sheet briefly, then cool completely on wire rack. Store in an airtight container. Makes two dozen cookies.

Serve *Mocha Meringue Stars* with *cafe mocha* or *espresso*.

*He said to them, "Come away by yourselves to a lonely place
and rest a while."* Mark 6:31 (NASB)

Solace in Solitude

Recipe: Hermits

I, John, your brother and companion in the suffering and kingdom and patient endurance that are ours in Jesus, was on the island of Patmos because of the word of God and the testimony of Jesus.

Revelation 1:9

John didn't plan the solitude he experienced on Patmos, but he still used it well to draw near to God. In the middle of John's loneliness and separation from loved ones, God visited him in a way unlike anything John had experienced before. God revealed the most intense vision recorded in Scripture when John was the most alone.

Everyone experiences loneliness at some time. Loneliness may come after a move to a new neighborhood or city. Loss often brings loneliness as well. It may be the loss of a parent, or it may be a newly empty nest. Changing jobs or changing churches can create a sense of being alone even in a crowd. While we may feel lonely and forgotten, we can be sure God doesn't forget us when we are lonely.

Joseph was imprisoned, yet God was with him and gave him the ability to interpret the dreams of others, which ultimately freed him. David felt alone while running from Saul, but he knew "though my father and mother forsake me, the LORD will receive me" (Ps. 27:10). The prophet Elijah received God's comfort after he delivered a message that prompted Jezebel to threaten to kill him. Jesus often sought solitude to talk intimately with his Father and to be refreshed before continuing his ministry.

Jesus calls us to solitude. We have lost our appreciation for quiet, and our ability to search for God in silent moments. In our noisy world we often seek to avoid silence. Our society tells us that having a full life means living with our senses filled all the time. Public places reverberate with background music. At home we often leave the radio or television on to avoid a sensation of aloneness. Brother Lawrence, in his classic *The Practice of the Presence of God,* said,

Solace in Solitude

"For the right practice of the presence of God, the heart must be empty of all other things."

A while back I realized my need to become more aware of God in the small moments of my life. It's one thing to *know* he's always there, but it's another thing to *notice* it. I decided to write down evidences of God at work in my life. At first it took focused effort, but after a few weeks, spotting God's presence and involvement in my daily life became a habit. Sometimes I found answered prayer, sometimes an unrequested blessing.

One subtle consequence of my intentional watching and listening for God was an absence of loneliness. A few months into my new habit, my husband took a short-term job that required him to work nights, between fifty and seventy hours a week. He slept during the day, which left about an hour every day that he was awake at home. The one-month assignment stretched into three, and I was alone a lot. But my solitude wasn't lonely, because of my new awareness of God's presence with me. When we moved to a new state two months later, I missed my friends and family but didn't experience the heartbreaking loneliness I had at other times.

"Because he has created us as unique individuals, our Father knows the best way to fill each one's empty places," says writer Gini Andrews. "It is only God who can fill our deep-est longings, who never has an appointment elsewhere, who never replaces us with someone he likes better, who promises never to leave us totally alone."[2] Once we take this to heart, we can see silence and solitude in a new light.

Father Henri Nouwen put it this way: "The more we train ourselves to spend time with God and him alone, the more we will discover that God is with us at all times and in all places. Then we will be able to recognize him even in the midst of a busy and active life."[3]

At times you may choose silence and solitude to enter God's presence. At other times you may find yourself alone and lonely. But you can learn to live in his presence by letting the silence remain and by listening for that still, small voice that always speaks of his love and care for you.

Hermits

This traditional American cookie can help you remember that God's presence and companionship are most real when you are most alone.

½ cup (1 stick) butter or margarine, softened
¾ cup packed brown sugar
1 egg
2 tablespoons milk
1 teaspoon vanilla extract
1½ cups flour
½ teaspoon baking soda
½ teaspoon ground cinnamon
¼ teaspoon ground nutmeg
⅛ teaspoon ground cloves
1 cup raisins or mixed, diced dried fruit
½ cup chopped walnuts or almonds

Preheat oven to 375 degrees. Lightly grease baking sheets.

In a large mixing bowl, beat together butter and brown sugar until fluffy. Beat in egg and milk. Add vanilla extract.

Add flour, baking soda, cinnamon, nutmeg, and cloves. Mix until thoroughly combined. Stir in raisins or fruit and nuts.

Drop by teaspoonfuls onto prepared baking sheets. Bake eight to ten minutes or until edges are lightly browned. Cool on a wire rack and store in an airtight container. Makes three dozen cookies.

Try *Hermits* with *your favorite coffee* and a cinnamon-flavored creamer.

I was hungry and you gave me something to eat, I was thirsty and you gave me something to drink, I was a stranger and you invited me in. Matthew 25:35

Rewarded Secrets

Recipe: Dark Secrets

There were no needy persons among them. For from time to time those who owned lands or houses sold them, brought the money from the sales and put it at the apostles' feet, and it was distributed to anyone as he had need. . . . Now a man named Ananias, together with his wife Sapphira, also sold a piece of property. With his wife's full knowledge he kept back part of the money for himself, but brought the rest and put it at the apostles' feet.

Then Peter said, "Ananias, how is it that Satan has so filled your heart that you have lied to the Holy Spirit and have kept for yourself some of the money you received for the land? Didn't it belong to you before it was sold? And after it was sold, wasn't the money at your disposal? What made you think of doing such a thing? You have not lied to men but to God."

Acts 4:34–35; 5:1–4

When you give to the needy, do not let your left hand know what your right hand is doing, so that your giving may be in secret. Then your Father, who sees what is done in secret, will reward you.

Matthew 6:3–4

Have you ever had someone offer to help you, yet they made you feel that you had to be so eternally grateful, you wish they hadn't even bothered? Or have you heard of someone who offered assistance, but they told so many people about their "act of charity" that the recipients were embarrassed because so many people now knew of their trouble?

These Scripture passages speak about giving without expecting recognition. They warn us to evaluate our motives, encouraging us to help others without making a big deal about it—to them or to others.

Often when we read Scripture that speaks of giving or caring for the needy, we think of the poor, the homeless, women and children on welfare, folks who are in need because of a fire or flood or famine. However, the needy aren't always the poor, and needs aren't always physical.

Mother Teresa, the nun known for her years of devotion to serving India's poorest in Calcutta, once said, "We may not have people hungry for a plate of rice or for a piece of bread in New York City, but there is a tremendous hunger and a tremendous feeling of unwantedness everywhere. And that is really a very great poverty."[4]

When my parents went into full-time ministry during my senior year of high school, raising support and getting the new work started didn't leave much money for the extra expenses that go with graduating from high school. Having moved and changed schools in the middle of the school year left me feeling rather anonymous in the midst of the festivities. In the weeks before commencement, one thing helped me feel a little less lost: graduation greetings from friends and family.

One plain white envelope stood out from the rest. It was a small, letter-sized envelope, not big enough to contain a card. It was addressed to me in unfamiliar handwriting and had no return address or other identifying information on the outside.

Inside was a simple piece of white paper folded around a twenty-dollar bill. A note con-

gratulated me on reaching this milestone and suggested that maybe I would need the money for a graduation dress. That gift was the most special one I received. It wasn't just the money but the fact that someone thought of me and cared enough to help meet a need.

Nearly twenty years later I still don't know who sent it. Maybe they enjoyed seeing me in my red graduation dress. Maybe they have no idea how they actually helped me. But I am sure that God blessed them for being a blessing to me.

There are as many ways to help the "poor" as there are types of "poverty." Maybe someone who is lonely needs an invitation to dinner or a cup of coffee. New parents may need an evening out together. A single mom may need the oil in her car changed. A latchkey child in the neighborhood might need cookies and milk after school.

If you see a need you can meet, you don't need to form a committee or start a new ministry. Without fanfare you can simply meet the need. The blessings will follow. It's a promise.

Dark Secrets

It's not always easy to do good things without wanting to receive some type of recognition. You can serve Dark Secrets *as a reminder that what you quietly do to meet the needs of others will not be forgotten by God.*

2 cups dates, pitted and chopped
1 cup pecans, chopped
1 cup flour
1 teaspoon baking powder
½ cup (1 stick) butter
1 cup brown sugar, packed
3 eggs
1½ teaspoons vanilla extract
powdered sugar

Preheat oven to 350 degrees. Grease and flour a nine-by-thirteen-inch pan.

In a large bowl, combine dates, pecans, flour, and baking powder. In a medium bowl, beat together butter and brown sugar until light. Beat in eggs and vanilla extract.

Add butter mixture to dry ingredients, beating until smooth.

Pour mixture into prepared pan and spread evenly. Bake eighteen to twenty minutes or until top is golden. Let cool in pan on wire rack for about ten minutes. Cut into bars, roll in powdered sugar, and store in an airtight container. Makes two dozen cookies.

Try *Dark Secrets* with a *vanilla nut-flavored coffee.*

God chose the weak things of the world to shame the strong.
1 Corinthians 1:27

Equipped for the Task

Recipe: Bear Paws

[David said,] "The LORD who delivered me from the paw of the lion and the paw of the bear will deliver me from the hand of this Philistine."

Saul said to David, "Go, and the LORD be with you."

Then Saul dressed David in his own tunic. He put a coat of armor on him and a bronze helmet on his head. David fastened on his sword over the tunic and tried walking around, because he was not used to them.

"I cannot go in these," he said to Saul, "because I am not used to them." So he took them off. Then he took his staff in his hand, chose five smooth stones from the stream, put them in the pouch of his shepherd's bag and, with his sling in his hand, approached the Philistine.

1 Samuel 17:37–40

You probably know the rest of the story. Everyone laughed at David, but the first stone he pitched hit Goliath right between the eyes, and he fell down dead.

David knew what the rest of the people didn't seem to understand: When God has selected you for a job, you don't always need special equipment. He will use what you have. He never asks you to do a job for which he hasn't equipped you.

Have you ever noticed how often God used the clearly unequipped to accomplish great things for him?

An elderly childless couple—he was one hundred years old and she was ninety. But God fulfilled his promise, and Abraham and Sarah became the parents of the nation of Israel.

A young man was sold into slavery by his brothers. God then used Joseph to save Egypt and the nation of Israel from famine.

An army of twenty thousand was reduced to three hundred. God used Gideon to lead this tiny army to victory over the mighty Midianites.

One disciple denied that he even knew Christ. Later Peter was used to establish the church.

If you look at most of our Christian leaders—past and present—you'll find many people from humble beginnings who allowed God to equip them for a work only he could imagine.

Equipped for the Task

Blind from six weeks of age, Fanny Crosby composed nearly nine thousand hymns and established patterns used in contemporary Christian music today.

Who would have imagined that a young man from a farm in North Carolina would become an international evangelist, drawing millions of people around the world to hear the gospel at his Billy Graham crusades?

When Joni Eareckson Tada was paralyzed from the neck down as a teenager, who would have imagined that God would make of her a renowned artist, best-selling author, singer, and radio personality and use her to establish an international ministry to the disabled?

Promise Keepers founder Bill McCartney says that he is the most unlikely choice to lead men back to their biblical roles. If he had let his sense of inadequacy hold him back, millions of families and hundreds of communities across America wouldn't be experiencing the blessings of lives committed to God's ways.

God imagined all of it. He has always been the God of the ineffective, the unfaithful, and the unlikely, gifting them with his power to accomplish his work for his glory.

Sometimes fear or a sense of our own inadequacy can threaten our resolve to follow through on an assignment from the Lord. When I started writing my first contracted book, during my last moments of consciousness before sleep and my first drowsy moments in the morning, I heard a message repeated daily: "You can't write a book. You can't write a book."

Throughout the months I worked on it, that message of fear continued to beat in my heart. On the one hand it could have been a message from the Enemy, sent to keep me ineffective, to prevent me from accomplishing the work God had given me to do. But at the same time it served as a reminder that, left to my own, I *couldn't* write that book. Yet with God's help and power, I could—and did. Once I had faithfully completed that first assignment, the message stopped. Even though I've written several books since then, it has never returned.

What has God asked you to do? The eleventh chapter of Hebrews lists the names of many who faithfully did what God asked, even though they couldn't see how they would accomplish it in the face of their limitations. God provides what we need to accomplish what he's planned for us. Our part is to accept the assignment in faith and follow the path he gives us, knowing that if we don't feel equipped for the task, we're probably headed in the right direction.

Bear Paws

David knew that the God who spared him from the paw of the bear would equip him even to kill a giant. You can serve Bear Paws *whenever you need to be reminded that God will equip you for what he asks you to do.*

1 cup ground almonds
2 cups powdered sugar
1 tablespoon unsweetened cocoa powder
¾ cup flour
pinch of salt

3 egg whites
2 ounces (2 squares) unsweetened
    chocolate, chopped fine
½ teaspoon almond extract
½ teaspoon vanilla extract

In a medium bowl, combine ground almonds, powdered sugar, cocoa powder, flour, and salt. Mix well. Add egg whites and beat until smooth. Add unsweetened chocolate and transfer to heavy saucepan or double boiler.

Cook over low heat, stirring constantly for five minutes or until chocolate is melted and mixture has thickened slightly. Remove from heat and stir in extracts.

Cover and refrigerate for one to two hours or until mixture has cooled and is stiff. Do not overchill or dough may be dry and hard to work with.

Preheat oven to 350 degrees. Line baking sheets with baking parchment.

To create bear paws, break off a teaspoonful of dough, roll into ball, and place on prepared sheet. Make three balls of ½ teaspoon dough. Place smaller balls close together on sheet along one side of large ball. Flatten slightly so all pieces are touching.

Continue with remaining dough, allowing about two inches between *Bear Paws* on cookie sheets.

Bake for twelve to fifteen minutes or until cookies have puffed and are somewhat crinkly and nearly firm to the touch. Allow cookies to cool for five minutes on baking sheets, then transfer to wire racks to cool. Makes two dozen cookies.

Serve these *Bear Paws* with an *almond- or chocolate-flavored coffee.*

Do everything without complaining or arguing, so that you may [be] without fault in a crooked and depraved generation, in which you shine like stars in the universe. Philippians 2:14–15

Filled with Light

Recipe: Pretty Eyes

The eye is the lamp of the body. If your eyes are good, your whole body will be full of light. But if your eyes are bad, your whole body will be full of darkness. If then the light within you is darkness, how great is that darkness!

Matthew 6:22–23

Isn't it curious: even with twenty-twenty vision, our eyes won't function if there is no light?

Have you ever been in a totally dark place? Once I went on a group tour of a cave in California. After winding our way through the cave for a while, we reached a large area underground where the guides had everyone turn off their lights. It was absolutely, completely dark—no cracks of light under the door, no moon or stars to illuminate anything.

After a minute or two to allow our eyes to adjust to the darkness, it was still impossible to see our own hands in front of our faces! It would have been impossible to safely find our way out of the cave. In the complete and utter darkness, though, the flame from a single match was enough to cast light throughout the cavern. But just a little light showed only a little of the vastness of what was there.

Have you ever noticed that the darker it is, the less color you can see? You may be able to see clearly enough to make out shapes, faces, and objects, but the full spectrum of color can't be exposed unless there is adequate light. In fact, it's been said that color does not exist apart from light.

I think that's an important fact to remember when we think about being the "light of the world." Do we have enough light within us that we can truly light up the world around us? Or do we have just enough light to keep people from bumping into things but not enough to show the true colors that exist?

Jesus said, "Let your light shine before men, that they may see your good deeds and praise your Father in heaven" (Matt. 5:16). It's easy to think that being a light means telling others about Christ. But when Jesus tells us to let our light shine, it's not simply words about our faith that he's interested in; it's our attitudes as well.

Filled with Light

As Cardinal John Henry Newman encouraged, "Let us seek the grace of a cheerful heart, an even temper, sweetness, gentleness and brightness of mind, as walking in his light, and by his grace."[5]

Catherine Marshall tells of an experiment that began when she was convicted by God that her speech was filled with too much criticism and harshness. She knew that she needed to break those deeply embedded habits. At first Catherine resisted the idea. She reasoned that God gave her the abilities to analyze and evaluate—shouldn't she use them to see situations as they really were? But knowing God was telling her otherwise, she agreed to be obedient. She decided to begin by not saying anything negative or critical for one day.

At lunch with her family, Catherine found that eliminating negative and critical comments from her conversation left her little to say. Even more surprising to her was that her family apparently didn't even notice. She said the experience left her feeling as if she "had been wiped out as a person." It was a sad acknowledgment of just how critical she had become.

Although it was difficult, as the hours passed she noticed positive changes taking effect. She found renewed humor and creativity and discovered that even her prayers were changed. While praying for a young friend who had wandered off course, Catherine saw a new, specific, uplifting request replacing her usual plea for God to fix the situation. The positive request brought a new sense of hope and joy to her prayer time. She admitted that the one-day experiment was not a quick fix, but she did vow to continue her "fast on criticalness."[6]

Have you noticed how much easier it is to focus on the negative? The news media is often maligned for reporting only the bad news. Even young children learn that they can generate laughter by being critical of others. And in our homes we often more quickly point out what others do wrong than what they do well. But as the nineteeth-century minister Frederick William Faber pointed out, "What can be more unkind than to communicate our low spirits to others, to go about the world like demons, poisoning fountains of joy? Have I more light because I have managed to involve those I love in the same gloom as myself?"[7]

We can bring more light into the world by eliminating our negative and critical talk and behavior. And like the flame in the cave, we will cast our glow to everyone who is near.

Pretty Eyes

This Turkish cookie can help you to remember that you'll really have "pretty eyes" if you allow the light of the Lord to shine through you by being a positive influence on those around you.

    1 cup (2 sticks) butter
    1 cup powdered sugar, sifted
    2 teaspoons vanilla extract
    2½ cups flour, sifted
    1 cup seedless raspberry or plum jam

Preheat oven to 350 degrees. Grease baking sheets or line with parchment.

In a large mixing bowl, beat butter until creamy. With electric mixer on low speed, gradually beat in powdered sugar. Beat about two more minutes, until very light and creamy. Beat in vanilla extract. Stir in flour.

Turn dough onto lightly floured surface. Knead dough until smooth. Use lightly floured rolling pin to roll dough ¼ inch thick.

Using three-inch round cutter, cut dough into circles. Using same cutter, make overlapping circles, cutting each round into two eye shapes (see photo). With apple corer or small round cutter, cut small circles in half of eye shapes.

Place cookies on prepared baking sheets. Bake ten to twelve minutes or until golden but not browned. Cool briefly on baking sheets, then cool completely on wire racks.

When cooled, spread center of whole cookies with jam. Place cookie with cutout on top, lightly pressing the two together.

Allow cookie to set for about one hour. Store in airtight container with parchment or waxed paper between the layers. Makes two dozen cookies.

Serve Pretty Eyes with your favorite coffee.

Whatever is true, whatever is noble, whatever is right, whatever is pure, whatever is lovely, whatever is admirable—if anything is excellent or praiseworthy—think about such things. Philippians 4:8

You Are What You "Eat"

Recipe: Fig Squares

No good tree bears bad fruit, nor does a bad tree bear good fruit. Each tree is recognized by its own fruit. People do not pick figs from thornbushes, or grapes from briers. The good man brings good things out of the good stored up in his heart, and the evil man brings evil things out of the evil stored up in his heart. For out of the overflow of his heart his mouth speaks.

Luke 6:43–45

My brothers, can a fig tree bear olives, or a grapevine bear figs? Neither can a salt spring produce fresh water.

James 3:12

When you hit your thumb with a hammer, how do you express yourself? What do you say when someone cuts you off in traffic or turns in front of you or "snakes" your parking spot? Are the words you speak when you're alone different from what you say when someone else is with you? Does your "act" hold up when you're hot or tired or hungry or stressed?

As kids, we were taught many principles about how we should speak and act:

"Think before you speak."

"If you can't say something nice, don't say anything at all."

"You catch more flies with honey than with vinegar."

"Garbage in, garbage out."

This last one seems to describe most clearly what the Scripture verses are saying: what we store up inside will eventually spill out somewhere.

What overflows out of your heart? It really does depend on what we take in. Just as our physical hearts can get clogged when we consume junk food, our spiritual hearts can get clogged when we consume junk books, music, movies, television, and even some conversations.

It's easy to say, "I'm not affected by the music; I don't really listen to the words." Yet after hearing a song just a couple of times, we find ourselves mindlessly singing along. Or we'll say that we know television shows aren't real, but then repeat a story line from a program to prove a point. What we take in really does come out—one way or another.

You Are What You "Eat"

When I was in high school, I saw this truth in my own life. Like most teenagers, I lived with the radio on. It didn't matter what was playing—I just surrounded myself with the popular music of the day.

Prior to my junior year, we moved to a new city, one with a Christian radio station. Most of the week the station broadcast talk shows and speakers, but on Sunday afternoons they played contemporary Christian music.

The more I listened to the Christian music, the less comfortable I was with secular music. I began to buy Christian music and listened to it more frequently.

After a while I noticed an attitude change. The more I listened to the negative messages of "junk" rock, the more impatient, argumentative, withdrawn, negative, and lonely I became.

As I listened to the music that taught Scripture and praised God, I found that I was more peaceful, less impatient, and more willing to act like a part of the family.

Writer Lynette Kittle had a similar response when she gave up watching soap operas. She said, "Once the negative input I'd been feeding on was removed, I noticed a 'cleaning up' of my own personal attitudes and outlooks."

The saying has been "What goes up must come down." It is also true that what goes in must come out. We are so careful about our diets. We eliminate fat, limit our sugar intake, eat in moderation, and eat natural foods without lots of additives. So what about what we take into our hearts and minds? Dr. Jan Dargantz says one way to evaluate movies, books, television, and other influences is to ask, "What is bad?" and "What do I need to know?"[8]

It isn't necessary to limit our music collections to classical music and hymns, or our television viewing to the history, nature, and news channels. But if we sometimes find ourselves saying things we wish we hadn't, we might need to look at what is going in and change our "diet." It could do our hearts good.

Fig Squares

Just as a fig tree, not a thornbush, bears figs, so the goodness that comes out of you is an overflow of the goodness you allow into your heart. You can serve Fig Squares *as a reminder of that truth.*

Filling:
1 pound dried figs, stems removed
1 cup brown sugar, packed
⅔ cup water
1 teaspoon vanilla extract

Crust:
1½ cups rolled oats (not instant)
1½ cups flour
1 cup brown sugar, packed
1 teaspoon cinnamon
½ teaspoon baking soda
½ cup walnuts or pecans, chopped
1 cup (2 sticks) cold butter, diced

In a medium saucepan, cook figs, brown sugar, water, and vanilla over medium heat until sugar is dissolved. With hand blender or food processor, blend until smooth. Set aside and allow to cool completely.

Preheat oven to 350 degrees. Grease and flour nine-by-thirteen-inch baking pan.

In a large bowl, combine oats, flour, brown sugar, cinnamon, baking soda, and nuts. Mix well. Using pastry blender or fingers, mix in butter until coarse crumbs form.

Spread half of crust mixture into prepared pan, pressing firmly to sides of pan. Pour cooled filling onto crust and spread evenly. Sprinkle remaining crust mixture evenly over filling.

Bake for thirty to thirty-five minutes or until crust is browned. Cool in pan on wire rack for one hour before cutting into squares. Store in airtight container. Makes two dozen bar cookies.

The sweet richness of *Fig Squares* goes well with a *hazelnut-flavored coffee,* or you can try *your favorite coffee roast* with a hazelnut-flavored creamer.

Humble yourselves before the Lord, and he will lift you up.

James 4:10

The Height of Humility

Recipe: Pride Cookies

To some who were confident of their own righteousness and looked down on everybody else, Jesus told this parable: "Two men went up to the temple to pray, one a Pharisee and the other a tax collector. The Pharisee stood up and prayed about himself: 'God, I thank you that I am not like other men—robbers, evildoers, adulterers—or even like this tax collector. I fast twice a week and give a tenth of all I get.'

"But the tax collector stood at a distance. He would not even look up to heaven, but beat his breast and said, 'God, have mercy on me, a sinner.'

"I tell you that this man, rather than the other, went home justified before God. For everyone who exalts himself will be humbled, and he who humbles himself will be exalted."

Luke 18:9–14

I worked one summer in the bookstore of a youth camp. During my first week a man came into the store and asked, "Do you have mine?" And he named the title of a book. I had only been there a couple of days and wasn't familiar with all the books yet. I had never seen the man before, and I thought he was asking for a book by an author named "Mein."

I could tell my puzzled look didn't please him. He went to the shelves, returned, and slapped a stack of books down in front of me. "I'm speaking here this week. You might want to have these on the counter."

Only after he left did I realize that he was the author of the book. I was offended at his prideful attitude but amused that he expected me to know who he was without any introduction.

That week he covered the usual camp topics—getting along with your family, dating and sexual purity, how Christ can change your life. Many students made decisions that week as he spoke eloquently of the value of a life lived for God.

I returned to camp the following year as a counselor and learned the same man who expected his reputation to precede him wherever he went had left his wife and family and abandoned his ministry to have an affair. His reported explanation, "I've given God his time; now it's my turn."

The Height of Humility

To most of us, that seems like an incredibly bold statement. But it's how much of our culture lives today—flat-out, in-your-face *pride*.

Proverbs 16:18—"Pride goes before destruction, a haughty spirit before a fall"—has been proved true many times over. I heard one speaker say that whenever he has seen a Christian leader fall, pride can be found at the bottom of the pile of troubles that led to the situation.

We don't think pride is a big deal anymore. Our society exalts those who exalt themselves and ignores those who don't seek the limelight. But as with all godly qualities, there is something within each of us that admires these traits when we see them.

After Tiger Woods won the Masters golf tournament, a *Reader's Digest* article about the young golf legend said the real reason he is so well liked is because he is humble and hardworking. Sadly, among sports heroes he's a real exception. In most sports it is the biggest and "baddest" (attitudes) that draw the most adoration. Young children wear the jersey numbers and copy the hairstyles of the most obnoxious players. People of all ages line up for autographs, and books detailing the sordid exploits of these "heroes" become best-sellers.

More drastic than the problem that pride can create among those *around* us is the problem it can create *within* us. The most common "religious" philosophy of this generation is that we hold all the answers within ourselves. Pride tells us that we hold our destiny in our own hands, so there is no need for God. The stronger we see ourselves, the less room we allow for God in our lives.

We seem to lose our perspective when, like the Pharisee, we compare ourselves with others around us. We look at our own good deeds or the amount of time that we spend praying or reading Scripture, and then we elevate ourselves above others who don't appear to measure up.

But what that tax collector knew, we need to realize as well. It doesn't matter how we compare with anyone else. It's not a matter of us reaching inside ourselves to find the good. Our true standing before God is the only thing that matters. And only when we recognize our inadequacy before God will he be able to work in our lives to strengthen our weaknesses. If we have a proper view of ourselves and of God, he will lift us up.

Pride Cookies

These treat-filled cookies can help you remember that you don't need to compare yourself with others or lift yourself up before God. He is more concerned with a right heart than with showy actions.

1 cup (2 sticks) butter, softened
1 cup brown sugar, packed
½ cup granulated sugar
2 teaspoons vanilla extract
2 eggs
2 cups rolled oats
1½ cups flour
1 teaspoon baking powder

1 teaspoon ground cinnamon
½ teaspoon ground nutmeg
½ teaspoon salt
1 cup toasted walnuts or almonds,
    chopped
1 cup coconut
1 cup chocolate chips (optional)

Preheat oven to 350 degrees. Grease or line two baking sheets.

In a large bowl, beat together butter and sugars until fluffy. Beat in vanilla and eggs, mixing thoroughly.

In a medium bowl, combine oats, flour, baking powder, cinnamon, nutmeg, and salt. Gradually add oat mixture to butter mixture, mixing thoroughly after each addition.

Stir in nuts and coconut and chocolate chips (if desired).

Drop tablespoonfuls of dough onto prepared baking sheets, two inches apart.

Bake ten to twelve minutes or until golden. Cool briefly on baking sheets, then transfer to wire racks to cool completely. Store in airtight container. Cookies also freeze well. Makes three dozen cookies.

Pride Cookies would go well with a true *Kona coffee*.

You are a shield around me, O Lord;
you bestow glory on me and lift up my head.   Psalm 3:3

Delight in Difficult Times

Recipe: Almond-Coffee Delights

Do not fret because of evil men
    or be envious of those who do wrong;
for like the grass they will soon wither,
    like green plants they will soon die away.

Trust in the LORD and do good;
    dwell in the land and enjoy safe pasture.
Delight yourself in the LORD
    and he will give you the desires of your
      heart.

Commit your way to the LORD;
    trust in him and he will do this:
He will make your righteousness shine like the
      dawn,
    the justice of your cause like the noonday
      sun.

Be still before the LORD and wait patiently for
      him;
    do not fret when men succeed in their ways,
    when they carry out their wicked schemes.
Psalm 37:1–7

Aren't we all drawn to the Scriptures that make great promises like "He will give you the desires of your heart"? But have you ever really looked at what comes before and after that promise?

"Do not ... be envious of those who do wrong."

"Be still before the LORD ... do not fret when men ... carry out their wicked schemes."

How is that possible?

My husband often jokes about my "over-developed sense of fairness." My whole family will agree that I never outgrew the "but that's not fair" phase.

While my head rebels against the idea of trusting, resting, delighting, and waiting while people get away with doing wrong around me, my heart knows the truth of these words.

Some years ago I was unexpectedly let go from a job. In the days and weeks following my departure, I learned of many untrue things that were being said about me. I wanted to set the record straight. I wanted to go to everyone who had misunderstood or misconstrued something and have them go to anyone they had told and restore my reputation.

Although that wasn't possible, I learned first-hand that God will defend and protect me. My fear that people would believe the untrue things was ungrounded. Because I had lived as honestly as I could before God, the truth came through. I didn't need to explain anything to anyone, and it didn't matter what "evildoers" had in mind for me. At times the waiting was agony, but I saw the truth that if I trusted in God, "he will make [my] righteousness shine like the dawn, the justice of [my] cause like the noonday sun." That's far more than I could ever have done on my own behalf!

I'm not the only one God has protected this way. A friend told of a pastor who was voted out of his church. Throughout the business meeting while members of the congregation were airing their opinions about him, he didn't speak out to defend himself, nor did he speak against those who were not behaving in a godly manner. Many people respected the way he conducted himself during those days. His new church is successful due in part, I'm sure, to the integrity that he exemplified.

I've also seen the consequences that come from a bold self-defense. I know of more than one situation in which someone felt they had been treated wrongly. They accused others of having evil intentions and made such a public spectacle of the situation that their own reputation suffered greatly. The Shakespearean line "Methinks the lady doth protest too much" must have come from a situation such as this. The more loudly we cry out that we've been wronged, the less convincing our argument becomes.

It's human nature to fight back. It doesn't make sense to sit still and wait. Yet so much of what God wants to teach us and do in us is contrary to human nature. That's because it's his nature that he wants to see grow in us.

When faced with an unfair situation, it helps to remember our greatest example—Jesus. He was unjustly accused, convicted, and sentenced to death. But "as a sheep before her shearers is silent, so he did not open his mouth" (Isa. 53:7). He even asked God to forgive the ones responsible.

It's easy to "delight . . . in the LORD" when everything is going well and our plans are succeeding. But we should remember that even when we're surrounded by evil, we can enjoy safe pasture and have the desires of our heart.

Almond-Coffee Delights

This rich cookie can be a reminder that you will be blessed when you delight in the Lord, even when your circumstances are less than delightful.

¾ cup butter or margarine, softened
⅓ cup granulated sugar
⅓ cup brown sugar, packed
1 teaspoon instant coffee dissolved in 2 tablespoons water
1½ cups self-rising flour
¾ cup (6 oz.) semisweet chocolate chips
½ cup chopped or slivered almonds

Preheat oven to 375 degrees.

In a large bowl, beat together butter and sugars until light and fluffy. Beat in the dissolved coffee.

Mix in flour, stirring until well blended. Stir in chocolate chips. Spread evenly on (nine-by-thirteen-inch) ungreased jelly roll pan or cookie sheet. Sprinkle almonds evenly over the top, pressing lightly into the dough.

Bake eighteen to twenty minutes or until cookies are nicely browned. Cool in pan on wire rack. When completely cooled, break into pieces. Store in an airtight container. Makes two dozen cookies.

Serve *Almond-Coffee Delights* with an *almond- or amaretto-flavored coffee* or creamer.

Jesus declared, "I am the bread of life. He who comes to me will never go hungry,
and he who believes in me will never be thirsty."   John 6:35

Spiritual Bread

Recipe: Coriander Diamonds

The manna was like coriander seed and looked like resin.

Numbers 11:7

"Our forefathers ate the manna in the desert; as it is written: 'He gave them bread from heaven to eat.'"

Jesus said to them, "I tell you the truth, it is not Moses who has given you the bread from heaven, but it is my Father who gives you the true bread from heaven. For the bread of God is he who comes down from heaven and gives life to the world."

John 6:31–33

Do you ever tire of the endless cycle required for our nourishment? Menu planning, clipping coupons, shopping, food preparation, cooking, eating, cleaning up, starting again? Do you ever find yourself bored with your meals? Do you search cookbooks for new ideas, try new things at restaurants so you can fix them at home, explore specialty markets for exotic ingredients to spice things up? Wouldn't it be nice to eat once, never to hunger again?

In the world today there is evidence of a great spiritual hunger. Covers of many national news publications have been dedicated to religious issues. One national television network has a dedicated religion correspondent covering the search for spiritual satisfaction in America. "Inspirational" books are the fastest-growing category in bookstores around the country. The *New York Times* best-seller list usually has at least one "spiritual" title.

I recently read one best-seller to see what the excitement was about. After almost two years it's still on the best-seller list and has spawned an abundance of supporting materials, gift items, and imitators. As I read, I discovered that the author was trying to help readers attain the life that we inherit when we follow God's plan. However, she was trying to do it without offering the genuine Source of that life. The same thing is true of most of these popular philosophies. They're spiritual meals with no substance.

This hunger of the heart is often treated the same way we treat our physical hunger: shopping around, searching both near and distant lands for the one sure cure to this deep emptiness.

Have you ever eaten a meal of "empty calories"? Chips, ice cream, cookies, soda. They can all be filling, but even though your stomach may be full, there are soon signals that your body needs more nourishment.

It's the same way with many of the spiritual paths offered today. The hype is exciting, and at times there is something that resembles truth or offers a glimpse of something that looks like God. But before long the effects of the sweetness are gone, and people are left filled but malnourished.

It has always been interesting to me to see what is the religious "flavor of the month." One "expert" will tell us to look inside ourselves, another will tell us the answer is to live a simple life, and yet another says that putting others first and meeting the needs around us is the answer.

Meanwhile people drift from one philosophy to the next, each time finding a brief respite, but soon that gnawing emptiness is back and the search resumes.

What many people don't realize is that it is Christ they are seeking. Living a simple life, serving others, and changing undesirable traits in ourselves are all fine goals, but that deep longing in the soul cannot be filled without God.

That is why the labels change and next month there will be a new lifestyle guru, with great hoards of people flocking to hear him or her speak. People will buy great quantities of books and tapes, only to try the next one the following month. One *Newsweek* magazine study found that many "seekers" who follow one particular guru will mix and match other philosophies as well. But if any of them really satisfied, no one would need to look any further.

Many books use the language of God, without acknowledging that only God can bring the fulfillment of everything our souls long for. No human philosopher can offer what Jesus did when he said, "I have come that [you] may have life, and have it to the full" (John 10:10).

Jesus, as the Bread of Life, can fill that hunger once and for all. If we've partaken of Jesus, we'll be warmed and filled, never to hunger again.

Coriander Diamonds

While the Israelites wandered in the wilderness, God satisfied their hunger with manna that "was like coriander seed." These unusual cookies can remind you of Jesus, the Bread of Life, who fills your spiritual hunger.

2 cups sugar
4 eggs, well beaten
1 cup almonds, chopped fine
3 cups flour
¼ teaspoon ground coriander
2 teaspoons ground cinnamon
1 teaspoon ground cloves

½ cup raisins or chopped dried fruit of choice
2 tablespoons melted butter
Glaze:
1 cup powdered sugar
¼ teaspoon almond extract
2 tablespoons milk

In a large mixing bowl, blend sugar and eggs until sugar is dissolved and mixture is smooth and creamy. Stir in almonds.

In a medium bowl, combine flour, coriander, cinnamon, and cloves. Gradually add flour mixture to sugar mixture, adding raisins or fruit after half of the flour. Stir until thoroughly combined.

Place dough on lightly floured board. Use rolling pin to roll to ¾-inch thickness. Using shape knife or pastry wheel, cut dough into diamond shapes.

Cover dough with clean kitchen towel. Allow to stand for several hours or overnight.

Preheat oven to 325 degrees. Place diamonds on ungreased cookie sheet, one inch apart. Brush tops with melted butter.

Bake twenty to twenty-five minutes or until golden. Cool on wire rack.

When cookies are lukewarm, spread with powdered sugar glaze, made by blending powdered sugar, almond extract, and milk. Let set for one hour before storing in airtight containers with waxed paper between the layers. Makes three dozen cookies.

You can try these *Coriander Diamonds* with *Turkish coffee.*

There is no difference, for all have sinned and fall short of the glory of God, and are justified freely by his grace through the redemption that came by Christ Jesus.   Romans 3:22–24

Come As You Are

Recipe: Biscotti

The woman was a Greek, born in Syrian Phoenicia. She begged Jesus to drive the demon out of her daughter.

"First let the children eat all they want," he told her, "for it is not right to take the children's bread and toss it to their dogs."

"Yes, Lord," she replied, "but even the dogs under the table eat the children's crumbs."

Then he told her, "For such a reply, you may go; the demon has left your daughter."

Mark 7:26–29

This was just the beginning of Jesus' ministry to many people who were deemed "unworthy" by the religious leaders of the time. Jesus came to help those who needed it the most: "It is not the healthy who need a doctor, but the sick" (Matt. 9:12). It's unfortunate that so many people miss this message.

The Syrian Phoenician woman understood it. Though Jesus' work had been only for the Jews up to that point, she knew that even as an outsider all she needed was the smallest part of Jesus' power—the "crumbs."

Jesus still works among those who are least likely. They are often the most receptive to the message of forgiveness and the fresh start that he offers. But sometimes the changes come slowly. As Eugenia Price explained, "God, who is always in motion toward us, working with us where we are and as we are, trusts his own power to change us day by day into his image."[9] Do we accept these people into the family while God does his work?

Rebecca Manley Pippert tells the story of Bill, a college student in the seventies. He was a "wild-haired" young man whose wardrobe was a torn T-shirt, jeans, and no shoes. After he gave his life to Christ, he decided to visit a church across the street from campus.

The people at the popular church were well dressed and conservative. Bill arrived late, and as he walked up the aisle, he realized there were no seats available. So he sat down on the carpet. It wasn't a problem for him, but the congregation was visibly uncomfortable.

As the tension grew, an elderly man, well dressed and dignified, made his way up the aisle toward Bill. The congregation watched breathlessly, expecting the older gentleman to ask the young man to move. Instead, with some difficulty, he joined Bill on the floor and worshiped with him there.[10] This elderly man demonstrated a true understanding of God's grace to us, and the importance of extending that same grace to others.

Our hearts are warmed by the realization that God desires to be with us just as we are. But we can be stingy in extending that grace to others, even though they are no less worthy. Do you know of people who say that they can't come to church or talk to God because they aren't "good enough"? How sad. So many people believe they have to be better people *before* they come to God. Just the opposite is true: only when we come to God can he make us better people.

My husband once had a job with a utility company. Having worked at a church for the previous seven years, it was quite an education. During the long shifts on the small crew, he began to see their spiritual hunger. Night after night discussions would turn to matters of the heart, with questions about where God fit into their lives.

One of the men mentioned that he would like to attend church, but he didn't think he was good enough. His wife and brother attended church, but he didn't think he could go until he quit smoking, cleaned up his language, and got some things under control at home.

Many people offer similar explanations when asked why they don't go to church. As they drive by churches on Sunday mornings, they see everyone in their nice clothes, smiling and being kind to one another. They look at themselves and see unhappiness and unkindness, questions and doubts. And they think there's no place for them at church until they conform to the image of everyone else. But as Eugenia Price puts it, "God does not wait for us to become perfect and in possession of only high, pure thoughts and unmixed motives before he moves through us."[11] As we gratefully accept God's gift of patience on our behalf, we should remember to offer his grace to others as well.

Biscotti

I've always thought that Biscotti *looks like the crusts of bread that kids sneak under the table to feed family pets.* Biscotti *can remind you that God's grace is for everyone. You don't have to wait until you're "good enough."*

½ cup (1 stick) butter
4 ounces semisweet chocolate
½ cup unsweetened cocoa
1½ cups all-purpose flour
1½ teaspoons baking powder
½ teaspoon salt

¼ teaspoon ground cinnamon
1 cup sugar
1 egg
1 teaspoon vanilla extract
sliced almonds (optional)

Preheat oven to 350 degrees. Grease and flour large baking sheet (and if you have them, two metal ice cube trays with the ice molds removed).

In the top of a double boiler (water should not touch bottom of upper pan), melt together butter and semisweet chocolate. Stir until well blended, and set aside to cool.

In a medium bowl, combine unsweetened cocoa, flour, baking powder, salt, and cinnamon. In a large bowl, beat together sugar and egg on medium speed until thoroughly mixed and pale in color. With mixer on low speed, beat in vanilla extract and the cooled chocolate mixture.

Gradually add the flour mixture. With hands, knead lightly to mix in crumbs of dough. (If you want almonds, add them now.) Turn onto lightly floured board and divide dough into two pieces. Shape into flattened logs. If you have the ice cube trays, place logs into prepared trays. Otherwise shape logs on prepared baking tray. Smooth tops of logs.

Bake for thirty minutes or until firm. Allow to cool in trays or on baking sheets for fifteen minutes. Remove logs to cutting board and carefully cut into ½-inch slices. Place the slices flat on the baking sheets and return to oven for five minutes. Turn slices and bake for five minutes on other side. Allow to cool on baking sheet. Makes two dozen *Biscotti*.

Biscotti is traditionally served with *espresso* or *cappuccino*, but these chocolatey *Biscotti* are delicious with *cafe mocha* or with *any other coffee* you'd like to dunk them in.

*Make plain to everyone . . . this mystery, which for ages past was kept hidden in God,
who created all things.* Ephesians 3:9

Dropping Clues
Recipe: Desert Mysteries

Surely you have heard about the administration of God's grace that was given to me for you, that is, the mystery made known to me by revelation, as I have already written briefly. In reading this, then, you will be able to understand my insight into the mystery of Christ, which was not made known to men in other generations as it has now been revealed by the Spirit to God's holy apostles and prophets. This mystery is that through the gospel the Gentiles are heirs together with Israel, members together of one body, and sharers together in the promise in Christ Jesus.

Ephesians 3:2–6

Throughout the Old Testament, from Adam to Zechariah, from Eden to the Promised Land, the plan of salvation was explained to the Jews. Every now and then, though, that plan included someone who wasn't a Jew—a Gentile.

Rahab, a prostitute in Jericho, hid the Israelite spies from the men who would certainly kill them. Because of her faith, she and her family were spared when the Israelites took over her city. Rahab became part of the lineage of Christ. Ruth, the great-grandmother of King David, from whose line Jesus came, was from Moab. She wasn't an Israelite. Perhaps God included people like Rahab and Ruth as a hint that ultimately he wanted all people to know him. The "chosen people," the Jews, were God's chosen pathway of salvation but not the only ones chosen to be saved.

Why is it important that we know Jesus' roots? What would have happened if Jesus had just appeared on earth without a human connection—without a lineage? Wouldn't it be difficult to accept him as a man who understands our struggles, as much as the God who understands our shortcomings?

Because we can trace his lineage, there is no question that Jesus was human. Because he conquered death and lives today, there is no question that he is God. And although the Jews were the chosen lineage, Jesus is for the entire world. It is that mystery we need to remember.

What exactly is a mystery? The first definition listed in the dictionary states, "A religious truth that one can know only by revelation and cannot fully understand." The second is more commonly used: "Something that baffles or perplexes; what cannot be fully understood by human reasoning."[12] In contemporary literature the term has been adapted to mean a story with a puzzle or riddle that won't be revealed until the end. There's something about a mystery that brings out the armchair detective in all of us.

C. S. Lewis describes going for a drive that began with questions and doubts in his mind and ended with an assurance that God was who he claimed to be and Jesus was the link between God and man. The moment he recognized this was the moment he placed his faith in the Lord.

Writer Laurel Lee Thaler describes a similar experience. The mystery was solved for her as a young woman homesteading in Alaska. As she read God's Word there in the wilderness, little by little God revealed himself to her until all the clues came together and she recognized her need for a Savior. She tells of going to sleep one evening and waking up the next morning with all the pieces fitting together and a new understanding in her heart.

Those of us who have had the pieces put together in a more deliberate fashion look at these types of experiences as mysteries themselves. We don't understand how someone could slowly drift from unbelieving to believing. But just as the truth of God being for all people was a mystery to the Jews, we need to recognize that God works in each heart in his own way. Those of us who put all the clues together a long time ago forget that it's a mystery because it's already been solved. Sometimes we overlook the many people around us who are missing clues—vital pieces of information needed to solve the puzzle and to understand God's place in their lives.

God has done his part, and Scripture is clear that as many as believe will come. But we must still be aware of opportunities to introduce him to others. There's no way of knowing exactly what someone needs to hear to understand God's plan. We can ask him to help us be more aware of the people around us to whom we can reveal additional clues.

Desert Mysteries

This light, rich cookie can be a reminder that Jesus came for all people. Serve them to help you remember to share pieces of this mystery with others you know.

    3 large egg whites
    ¼ teaspoon cream of tartar
    ¼ teaspoon almond extract
    ¾ cup sugar
    ¾ cup almonds, chopped
    ¾ cup dates, pitted and chopped

Preheat oven to 250 degrees. Line baking sheets with parchment.

In large mixing bowl, beat egg whites, cream of tartar, and almond extract on medium speed until foamy.

Gradually beat in the sugar, beating until stiff and glossy. Gently fold in almonds and dates.

Drop by teaspoonfuls onto prepared baking sheets, about one inch apart.

Bake twenty-five to thirty minutes or until just firm to the touch and pale in color.

Cool on wire racks. Store in airtight containers. Makes four dozen cookies.

Desert Mysteries are nice with an *almond-flavored coffee.*

He has made everything beautiful in its time.
Ecclesiastes 3:11

Metamorphosis

Recipe: Cinnamon Butterflies

Therefore, if anyone is in Christ, he is a new creation; the old has gone, the new has come!

2 Corinthians 5:17

It was one of those perfect spring days. The cloudless blue sky sparkled the color of aquamarines. The air was sweet with the scent of jasmine and roses. I walked along, satisfied and inspired by an afternoon at my favorite cafe, hearing only the songs of birds and the buzzing of industrious insects.

As I admired the beautiful magenta color of a bougainvillea in full bloom, out of the corner of my eye I noticed something flying toward me. If my arms hadn't been loaded down with books, I probably would have swatted at what I first perceived to be some sort of nasty bug. But as I turned, I saw a butterfly. Instantly sorry for having such violent thoughts, I was glad I had not acted on my impulse to send the annoyance on another flight path.

The butterfly continued on its way, and I on mine. As I thought about the near calamity, I wondered why it is that we have such a natural aversion to insects of almost every sort, but butterflies are somehow set apart from human interference.

It could be because they're prettier than most bugs. They look a little like flowers on the wing. They don't bite, so we don't have that instinctive reaction to repel them at all cost. They are known to dine on many of our favorite garden plants, but even that isn't enough to incite violence toward the fragile creatures. Even in their pre-beauty stage as caterpillars we tend to leave them alone, allowing them the chance to develop into their colorful potential.

Perhaps we leave them alone because they're the ultimate "ugly duckling" story. Butterflies give us hope. They won't always be like hairy worms, crawling in the dirt, hoping to avoid cats and careless footsteps until they can be transformed into beautiful soaring creatures.

Butterflies were the subject of one of my earliest science lessons. Someone found a caterpillar, and my third-grade teacher put it into a jar with holes poked in the lid. A good supply of mulberry leaves was included (we were told they like mulberry leaves the best), and daily we watched to see what was going to happen.

The hairy black caterpillar busied itself eating leaves for energy and shedding its skin to form a chrysalis on one of the branches in the jar. After a couple of days the caterpillar had disappeared completely into its new leaf-green home with the gold trim around the top.

Mrs. Walker told us that the caterpillar was still inside, changing into a butterfly. It didn't seem possible that the fat, hairy creature could build itself that tiny green house and come out as an orange and black monarch butterfly. It was easier to believe that Clark Kent could go into a phone booth and come out as Superman.

Days and days went by. It looked as if nothing were happening. Until one day someone noticed the chrysalis stirring just a bit. As we watched with renewed interest, the chrysalis broke open, and the wet, fragile butterfly emerged. It took a while for the damp wings to unfold completely. The butterfly opened and closed its wings until they were dry and strong and it was ready to fly. We learned that if we had helped it out of the cocoon or helped it dry its wings, it wouldn't have been able to fly. We took the jar outside, removed the lid, and watched as the wonderful creature flew off to its new life.

Just as only God could create a beautiful creature from a homely, fat, wormlike beginning, only God can take us from our ugly beginnings and transform us into new creatures that reflect his glory.

Something within us understands what it's like to start life unlovely. Once we understand the work God wants to do within us, we shed our old nature and emerge transformed into something altogether new and beautiful.

There are times when, like a child, we can be impatient, wanting the new creature to be revealed before it's ready. Or we want to help a newly freed creature of God gain its strength and take its first flight quickly. But interference with the built-in timetable can prevent the new creature from being able to fly at all. Fortunately, God always knows exactly how much time and attention we need, and he gives us everything it takes to "fly" right on schedule.

Whenever we see a butterfly, we can pause to remember our own humble beginnings and thank God for transforming us into something beautiful.

Cinnamon Butterflies

This simple cookie starts with a simple, utilitarian piecrust and transforms it into a sweet, beautiful treat. Enjoy these Cinnamon Butterflies *as a reminder that God can take your plain, unattractive life and transform it into something beautiful.*

> Piecrust: use either a favorite recipe or packaged crust, or
>   use crust left over from other baking
> 1 to 4 tablespoons soft butter or margarine
> ¼ cup granulated sugar
> 2 teaspoons cinnamon

Preheat oven to 325 degrees. Lightly grease baking sheet or line with parchment.

On a lightly floured surface, roll piecrust into a rectangle, about ¼ inch thick. Spread with softened butter or margarine. Combine sugar and cinnamon and sprinkle evenly over buttered crust.

Starting on the long side of the dough, roll jelly-roll style into a log. Flatten the log slightly so it is oval-shaped rather than round.

Cut log into one-inch slices with a knife, or use thread or dental floss, sliding the thread under the log, crossing ends over the top, and pulling until it is sliced through.

Unroll top of each one-inch roll just slightly, so there is about ½ inch of dough not tightly rolled with the rest. Make two connected rolls by cutting the one-inch slices in two, leaving the unrolled layer of pastry uncut.

Place on lightly greased baking sheet. Open slices so they lay flat with uncut section in the middle. With fingers, slightly crimp the sides of the slices to create the look of butterfly wings.

Bake for about eight to ten minutes or until crust is just golden. Cool on wire racks and store in an airtight container. Makes two dozen butterflies.

Cinnamon Butterflies are delicious with *cafe cinnamon.*

Notes

[1] Jill Briscoe, *Renewal on the Run: Encouragement for Wives Who Are Partners in Ministry* (Wheaton, Ill.: Shaw, 1992).

[2] Gini Andrews, *A Violent Grace* (Grand Rapids: Zondervan, 1986).

[3] Henri Nouwen, *The Way of the Heart* (San Francisco: HarperSanFrancisco, 1981).

[4] Mother Teresa of Calcutta, *My Life for the Poor* (New York: Harper & Row, 1985).

[5] Mary W. Tileston, ed., *Joy and Strength* (New York: Grossett & Dunlap, 1928).

[6] Catherine Marshall, *A Closer Walk* (New York: Avon, 1994).

[7] Tileston, *Joy and Strength*.

[8] Jan Dargantz, *Simple Truths: How You Can Teach Your Children the Twleve Most Important Lessons in Life* (Nashville: Nelson, 1995).

[9] Eugenia Price, *God Speaks to Women Today* (Grand Rapids: Zondervan, 1964).

[10] Rebecca Manley Pippert, *Out of the Saltshaker and into the World* (Downers Grove, Ill.: InterVarsity Press, 1979).

[11] Price, *God Speaks to Women Today*.

[12] *Webster's Collegiate Dictionary* (Springfield, Mass.: 1997).